Ex Libris
Thomas J. Frey

P9-CMS-946

PIOUS AND
SECULAR AMERICA

Books by Reinhold Niebuhr

THE SELF AND THE DRAMAS OF HISTORY

CHRISTIAN REALISM AND POLITICAL PROBLEMS

THE IRONY OF AMERICAN HISTORY

FAITH AND HISTORY

THE CHILDREN OF LIGHT AND THE CHILDREN OF DARKNESS

THE NATURE AND DESTINY OF MAN (ONE-VOLUME EDITION)

AN INTERPRETATION OF CHRISTIAN ETHICS

MORAL MAN AND IMMORAL SOCIETY

BEYOND TRAGEDY

Reinhold Niebuhr

PIOUS AND
SECULAR
AMERICA

New York

CHARLES SCRIBNER'S SONS

© 1958 BY REINHOLD NIEBUHR

A. 2-58 [H]

ALL RIGHTS RESERVED. NO PART OF THIS BOOK
MAY BE REPRODUCED IN ANY FORM WITHOUT
THE PERMISSION OF CHARLES SCRIBNER'S SONS.

PRINTED IN THE UNITED STATES OF AMERICA

LIBRARY OF CONGRESS CATALOG CARD NUMBER 58-5721

Four of the essays in this volume appeared first in the following magazines: *Confluence* and the *Yale Review;* Chapter 1
appeared in *The Atlantic Monthly* under the title "Piety
and Secularism in America" and Chapter 6 in *The Reporter*
under "A Theologian's Comments on the Negro in America."
Copyright 1956, 1957 by Reinhold Niebuhr.

FOR
Elisabeth

CONTENTS

PREFACE   vii

1. PIOUS AND SECULAR AMERICA   I

2. FRUSTRATION IN MID-CENTURY   14

3. HIGHER EDUCATION IN AMERICA   24

4. RUSSIA AND AMERICA: A STUDY IN
   HISTORICAL CONTINGENCY   39

5. LIBERTY AND EQUALITY   61

6. JUSTICE TO THE AMERICAN NEGRO FROM STATE,
   COMMUNITY AND CHURCH   78

7. THE RELATIONS OF CHRISTIANS AND JEWS
   IN WESTERN CIVILIZATION   86

8. THE IMPULSE FOR PERFECTION AND THE IMPULSE
   FOR COMMUNITY   113

9. MYSTERY AND MEANING   123

   INDEX OF PROPER NAMES   147

PREFACE

Most of the essays in this volume are journalistic and they, therefore, may be dated as all journalism is. But I can claim for them that all have been written or published in the years 1956 and 1957. Therefore, they will not require the reader to reconstruct the historical mood of decades in order to understand the essays; but since history moves very fast, even such recent essays may be obviously dated. I do not think, however, that the thesis of the essay on "America and Russia," for instance, has been invalidated by the recent surprising news of Russian technical advances and that the thesis of the essay on the race problem has been changed by what happened in Little Rock, Arkansas.

Most of the essays are published for the first time in this volume. Of the unpublished essays, the one entitled "The Relation of Christians and Jews in Western Civilization" was read as a paper before the joint meeting of the faculties of the Jewish Theological Seminary and Union Theological Seminary. "Mystery and Meaning" is based on sermons preached at Union Seminary and Harvard University.

Of the essays previously published, the first one, from which the collection takes its title, was published by the *Atlantic Monthly* in 1957 in their 100th Anniversary Issue. "Higher Education in

America" was published by *Confluence,* a quarterly journal of the Harvard Summer School. It was a part of a symposium on higher education in various nations. The essay on race relations in America was published by *The Reporter* in November 1956. "Liberty and Equality," a study of the political and social ethics of Britain, France and America, was published by the *Yale Review* in September 1957. I am grateful to these journals for the permission to republish these essays.

The reader will observe that the unity in this collection of essays is given by the primary interests of the author in the relationship of the religious to the social and political life of America. All the essays, with the exception of the two final ones, are devoted to various aspects of this interest.

REINHOLD NIEBUHR

PIOUS AND
SECULAR AMERICA

I

PIOUS AND SECULAR
AMERICA

The coexistence of the "godly" and the "godless" of traditional piety and modern secularism has been a characteristic of Western civilization since the seventeenth and eighteenth centuries. The rise of modern science created a rift in a traditionally Christian civilization and generated a "secular" spirit, which was denounced by the pious as heresy and which was welcomed by the "enlightened" as the harbinger of a promising future for mankind, as the guarantor of every private virtue and public justice. Neither party was able to annihilate the other as simply as it had hoped. Western civilization, thereupon, became the realm of very interesting forms of interpenetration and cooperation, some advertent and some inadvertent, between piety and secularism. But in no nation has this coexistence brought more remarkable results than in our own. For here we are in the twentieth century, at once the most religious and the most secular of Western nations. How shall we explain this paradox? Could it be that we are most religious partly in consequence of being the most secular culture? That would add a special depth to the paradox.

Let us begin by defining our terms. We are "religious" in the sense that religious communities enjoy the devotion and engage the active loyalty of more laymen than in any nation of the Western world. We are "secular" in the sense that we pursue the immediate goals of life, without asking too many ultimate questions about the meaning of life and without being too disturbed by the tragedies and antimonies of life. Our secularism is of two varieties. There is a theoretic secularism which dismisses ultimate questions about the meaning of existence, partly because it believes that science has answered these questions and partly because it regards the questions as unanswerable or uninteresting. There is a practical secularism, which expresses itself in the pursuit of the immediate goals of life. Our detractors in Europe and Asia think that our practical secularism expresses itself in "materialism" that is in the pursuit, not of happiness, but of comfort and physical security against all the hazards of nature and of history. If there should be a measure of truth in this charge, it would add a peculiarly ironic note to our contest with communism. For we profess to be "Godly" and the communists are philosophical materialists, who think that piety deflects men from seeking the obvious goods of life successfully. But our "Godly materialism" has been immeasurably more successful than their "godless" variety. One must hasten to add that not our piety, but our secular and scientific proficiencies, have greatly contributed to our superiority over the communist pursuit of happiness.

Actually, our detractors are not quite right in accusing us of "materialism." Our passion has been technical efficiency. We have been able to give ourselves to technics with greater abandon than any other nation. We are uninhibited by the traditional restraints upon the technical enterprise which obtained in European nations, including the first industrial nation of Europe, Britain. This passion for technical efficiency, together with the natural resources of a richly endowed continent and the advantages of a single continental economic unit, has given us a cornucopia. We are not displeased with the fruits of this cornucopia. They were not, however, the first concern of our enterprise. That was efficiency. We are somewhat embarrassed by the fact that we are the first culture which is in danger of being subordinated to its economy. We have to live as luxuriously as possible in order to keep our productive enterprise from stalling.

If religion has not only survived, but gained a new relevance in this secular environment, this curious development must be partly attributed to the limitations of both a theoretic and practical secularism. A theoretic secularism is inclined to hold the pursuit of happiness as the final meaning of life. This pursuit of happiness easily degenerates into the pursuit of comfort and security. But a culture which gives itself wholeheartedly to these ends is bound to discover the limits of this frame of meaning for the life of man.

Not all, but many, forms of secularism try to comprehend human life in a too simple frame of meaning. They may not equate happiness with comfort and security; but they usually do not appreciate those dimensions of human striving in which joy and sorrow are curiously blended and achieve, not happiness, but fulfillment. American secularism, following the French Enlightenment, makes much of the "dignity of man." But it is usually oblivious to the "misery of man," which is equally, with his dignity, the undoubted fruit of the unique freedom, which distinguishes him from the brutes. For the same freedom which makes man historically creative also gives him the capacity to be destructive and lifts him above natural vicissitudes to contemplate the vanity and brevity of life with melancholy. This glorious human creature undoubtedly dies as the animals do; but he is anxious about his life and his death. All the advances in medical science offer no cure for senility, or materially alter the brevity of human existence.

To the misery of human frailty and brevity one must add the perplexities of a guilty conscience. They cannot be eliminated simply by living a "blameless" life; for our responsibilities involve us in guilt. No one anticipated in the nineteenth century that the responsibility of saving our civilization would involve us in the guilt of risking an atomic war. We do much evil in order to do good. Furthermore, there are forms of guilt which cannot be reduced to the proportions of neurotic guilt, subject to psychiatric ministrations. There are of course forms of neurotic guilt feelings which require psychiatric attention.

It is because a philosophy of the enlightened mind and a civilization of great technical power cannot solve these ultimate problems of human existence that the frame of meaning, established by the traditionally historic religions, has become much more relevant to the modern man than seemed possible a century ago. There is in these religions a sense of mystery and meaning, which outrages the canons of pure rationality but which makes "sense" out of life. Our national culture was not only more completely devoted to the promises of nineteenth-century culture (the so-called "century of hope"), but it was more efficient in fulfilling the prescriptions for happiness than any other nation. The reaction to unful-

4

filled hopes is correspondingly more obvious. This is particularly true because we are subject not only to the perennial antinomies and tragedies of life which our enlightenment and our technical efficiency have not been able to overcome; but we are, as a nation, subject to frustrations in the days of our seeming omnipotence which we did not foresee in the days of our national weakness and innocence. We are less the masters of our fate in this day of American power than when we were still rocked in the cradle of continental security. The whole drama of history is evidently more mysterious and meaningful, even as individual existence, more filled with beauty and terror than the secular philosophies anticipated.

The non-technical cultures of Asia and Africa will naturally regret the premature religious resignation which contributed to their technical backwardness and will try to achieve a more rational understanding of the complexities of life and a more adequate technical conquest of nature. But we have travelled that path of progress almost to its limit. The religious quest of ultimate meanings was, therefore, bound to gain new relevance among us.

These facts do not, of course, preclude the possibility that the religious revival in our day may contain elements of rather frantic pursuits of the secular ends of "success" or "power" and represent religious versions of "secularism." In the current debate between piety and secularism it is always well to bear in mind that neither piety nor enlightenment are as simply the guarantors of either private goodness or public virtue as the proponents of each side contend. The cooperation between secularism and piety has been fruitful on the whole because each side possessed more common virtue than the opponent was willing to admit. Partly, each side had a unique virtue which prevented the other side from pursuing its characteristic virtues so consistently that they degenerated into vices. The democracy of the whole of Western civilization, including our own, is obviously the fruit of such cooperation.

Genuine piety sets up an authority for the individual conscience which prevents the state or the community from becoming an idolatrous end of human existence. Religious faith makes a rigorous affirmation, "We must obey God, rather than men," in opposition to all tyranny. But, unfortunately, piety develops its own idolatries by claiming a too simple alliance between the divine will and human ends. The soberness of a secular pursuit of immediate ends and a tolerant appreciation of the fragmentariness of all human viewpoints is necessary for the "limited warfare" of parliamentary democracy. This spirit of tolerance and the contrasting spirit of fanaticism may each be the fruits of either religious piety or rational enlightenment, contrary to the assumption of each side that the evil fruit is the product of the other side and the good fruit the characteristic consequence of our own world view. It is as rare an achievement for the pious man to be charitable as for the rational man to be "reasonable." Both achievements depend upon the recognition of the limited character of each one's vision of the truth.

Another religious reaction to a secular civilization has been developed in an unusual degree in America. Technical civilizations create great urban centers in which the individual is in danger of losing his identity in the crowd, gathered together by technics, but lacking the virtues of genuine community. Some of the current popularity of religion in our nation is undoubtedly due to the fact that religious congregations have

6

been able to establish integral communities in the impersonal
and technical togetherness of our urban centers. In these
communities, the individual comes to his own as a person
and lives in an environment of faith in which the vicissitudes
of his existence are understood. It is interesting that Americans are a more urban people than Europeans. They do not
require roots in the country as do most Englishmen. It is also
interesting that this urbanness has increased, rather than diminished, loyalty to the religious communities, though it was
previously assumed that religious faith flourished in the coun-
tryside and withered in the sophisticated city. This did not
prove to be so in America. The reason was probably that
religious faith was, in more ways than one, used as an anti-
dote to the simple meanings and fulfillments of a technical
culture.

Two very different types of religious congregations, both
uniquely American, contributed to the vitality of religious
loyalty in our nation. And both also contributed to the
uniquely American religiosity, which was at once more vital
and more "secular" than European religion. The one was the
sectarian church and the other the immigrant church. The
sect-church represented an exclusive religious community in
Europe, emphasizing voluntary membership, lay responsibility, and a critical attitude toward all the traditional "means
of grace" in the church, the sacraments, liturgies and theolo-
gies, and professional ministers, and an emphasis upon religious immediacy and personal religious "experience." The
radical sect, whether individualistic or socially radical, always
remained a minority group in Europe as compared with the
churches of inclusive membership, and frequently lived under
direct state auspices. In America, this sect conquered the

7

frontier. Its religious immediacy and the mobility of its quasi-lay leadership (the Methodist circuit rider, for instance) was suited to the frontier. On the frontier, the sect became the dominant church in America. The traditional churches remained in their urban settings. But in less than a century, the sect-churches colored the religious climate of the whole of America. In a sense, every church became a sect, at least in terms of emphasis upon lay responsibility and integral religious fellowship. The Methodist and Baptist churches are numerically the dominant churches in America. Most of them have grown respectable and only show vestigial remnants of the charismatic power by which they conquered the frontier.

But the same sect which revitalized religious life in America also "secularized" religious faith and prompted the criticism of European Christians, even to this day, that American faith is "secularized." What validity did this charge have? Over a century ago, De Toqueville, that perceptive French observer of the American scene, affirmed that the evangelical preachers of the American frontier were highly pragmatic in their exposition of their religion. They did not envisage "eternal felicity" as the end of the religious quest, he said, but rather commended religion as an aid in the pursuit of worldly ends such as "prosperity" and "civic peace and righteousness."

This disavowal of "otherworldliness" will seem very natural to American observers even today; but it was, unfortunately, accompanied by the frontier's rather sentimental "thisworld-liness," that is by the hope that the frustrations of life, as known in the old world would disappear on the frontier where "liberty and equality" seemed for the first time realizable ideals. Thus, the Enlightenment and evangelical Christianity

8

were merged on the American frontier and the result was that note of sentimentality which has characterized both political and religious thought in our nation ever since. "If one compliments an American," declared De Toqueville, "on the virtues of American life, he will take the compliment for granted and enlarge upon the vices and corruptions of European nations." The heaven of evangelical Christianity and the utopia of the Enlightenment were, thus, blended on the frontier. But utopia was uppermost in the imagination of the frontier. And it was an achieved utopia, not a future one. America was a kind of Kingdom of God. The final spiritual fruit of this frontier religious sentimentality came a century later when the "social gospel" thought the problems of life, including those of a technical civilization, would be solved if only people could be persuaded to love one another. The recalcitrance of human nature, expressed in St. Paul's well-known confession, "the good that I would do, I do not do; and the evil that I would not, that I do," is obscured in this sentimentality and all the hard problems of achieving justice in a community of self-seeking men are made easy by these hopes. Thus, a great thinker of the social gospel could say at the beginning of this century: "The impulse to give justice is evangelical; but the impulse to get justice is not. There is an ominous desire to get justice which reveals that we have lost confidence in spiritual forces."

Thus, a dissipated evangelicalism relied on "love," while the Enlightenment relied on "reason" to achieve utopia on earth. But both the secular and the religious version of utopianism denied the real problems of human existence and expected dreams to turn into reality cheaply. That is why the religious revival in America is only partly a reaction to

9

disappointed secular hopes and is partly a religious expression of those same hopes. Nothing could illustrate the bewildering confusion of secularism and religiosity in our nation more vividly. Perhaps we are so religious because religion has two forms among us. One challenges the gospel of prosperity, success, and achievement of heaven on earth. The other claims to furnish religious instruments for the attainment of these objectives.

The other unique American religious force which made a community for the individual in the anonymity of the urban center was the church of the immigrant. America was refashioned by the hordes of immigrants which came to our shores in the latter part of the nineteenth and the early part of the twentieth centuries. They brought their churches along with them. These churches, Catholic, Protestant, and for the Jews the synagogue, were anchored in a culture in the land of the immigrants' birth. But in the American environment, they became exclusive, and without organic relation to the American culture. They generated much more lay activity than in Europe and became fellowships which performed the function of guarding the immigrant against the anonymity of an urban and strange culture and of preserving something of the old world culture, including the language of the immigrant.

According to the thesis of Will Herberg's sociological analysis *Protestant, Catholic, Jew,* the immigrant church proved a very ready instrument both for preserving and for adapting the culture of the immigrant to America. For the church became the means of his self-identification without a too-obvious connotation of foreignness. The church was recognized as part of the "American way of life" and yet it was reminiscent of the culture of the home country. The immigrant church was, thus, popular for other than purely religious reasons. In a different way than the sectarian church, it pursued religious interest for essentially secular reasons and thereby became another instrument for the curious mingling of secularism and piety in America.

It must be added that the members of these immigrant churches were attracted to America, partly by its free institutions but mostly by its economic opportunities. These immigrants were first employed as poorly paid workers in our expanding economy. But in time, many of them rose into the managerial and owning class. Their religious faith did not inhibit them from pursuing the goals of economic well-being with absolute devotion. It may have actually supplied the discipline by which the economic activity could be more successfully engaged in. Thus, the immigrant church, together with the sectarian church was at one and the same time a refuge from a secular culture, and a resource for the uninhibited pursuits of essentially secular ends of life.

Thus, the religion of the immigrant achieved the same relation to secular ends in a few generations, which required a century of development in New England, where the original Puritanism was transmuted into "Yankeeism" of the New England business man.

If this analysis of the unique relation of piety to secularism in our own nation is at all correct, it becomes apparent that we are more religious and more secular than any other nation, not by accident, but by the effect of definitely ascertainable historic causes peculiar to the American experience. If the results are extravagant, it is always possible to console ourselves that the interpenetration of piety and secularism in our culture has been more creative in the political sphere than in the economic realm. In that sphere the secular devotion to immediate ends and the religious apprehension of ultimate authority, beyond the realm of the political order, have saved us from both the authoritarian politics of traditional piety and from the totalitarian politics of a consistent secularism, as developed historically from the French Revolution to the Russian Revolution.

In our economic life, we may have extravagantly pursued the immediate ends of life with such consistency that religion tended to become both a refuge against the anonymous social togetherness of an urban society, a balm for the inevitable disillusionments in which the rational and the technical "pursuit of happiness" is bound to end and (occasionally) a pious version of the secular pursuit.

The striking contrast between the relatively creative interpenetration of secularism and piety in our political life and the comparatively uncreative relation between the two in our economic life deserves a closing word.

We have seen that political democracy depended upon both piety and secularism, each contributing its characteristic insights to the organization of a free society. Secularism furnished the immediate and proximate goals of justice and prevented religion from confusing immediate with final goals of life, and, thus, developing its own idolatries. Piety, on the other hand, gave the individual a final divine authority, which enabled him to defy tyrannical political authority.

In the realm of economics, on the other hand, an efficient economy was the product of a secularism, which began by regarding happiness as the final end of life, continued by substituting comfort and security for happiness and ended by regarding efficiency as an end in itself. The idolatry which substituted a means to an end as the final end of existence has tended to vulgarize our culture. Piety has not essentially challenged this vulgarity or futility. Sometimes it has provided asylums of fellowship for the victims of the cult of efficiency; sometimes it has been a resource for further efficiency; and only occasionally it has challenged the inadequacy of these immediate goals as containing the final goals of life and a fulfillment of the meaning of human existence.

Our gadget-filled paradise suspended in a hell of international insecurity certainly does not offer us even the happiness of which the former century dreamed. Only when we finally realize the cause of these disappointed hopes can we have a truly religious culture. It will probably disappoint the traditionally pious as much as the present paradise disappoints the children of the Enlightenment.

In that event piety will have recaptured some of the characteristic accents of the historic religions, which, in their traditional form, may have regarded historic existence too much as a "vale of sorrows" but which had the virtue of knowing that there could be no complete happiness in human life because a creative life could never arrive at the neat harmonies which are the prerequisite of happiness. They knew that all human virtue remains fragmentary and all human achievements remain tentative. They knew that the meanings of life were surrounded by a penumbra of mystery and that life's joys and sorrows are curiously mingled. The great historic religions, in short, were rooted in the experiences of the ages so that they could not be deluded by the illusions of a technical age.

2

FRUSTRATION IN
MID-CENTURY

How do Americans react to the frustrations of this mid-century politically and religiously?

The frustrations and disappointments can be briefly described. While we enjoy a standard of living which is beyond the dreams of avarice of even the optimist among our forefathers, this prosperity is in sharp contrast to our insecurity in an atomic age. The peace we have is due to a nuclear stalemate between the two great power blocs into which the world has become divided; and each must make frantic efforts to preserve the stalemate by matching the achievements of the other in bombs and guided missiles.

This situation not only disappoints all the hopes which the two previous centuries had for us; it disappoints the hopes which we had for ourselves only a decade ago. At the close of the War, the United Nations Charter organized the nations of the world and made the possibility of unanimity among the great powers in the Security Council the basic assumption of the organization. In other words, this very non-utopian document failed to estimate the degree of recalcitrance, to which the communist creed would prompt the Russian giant. Roosevelt thought he could beguile Stalin by occasionally siding with him against Churchill; and Eisenhower assured our Congress, on return from his triumphs in Europe, that we and the Russians understood each other on the basis of our common "anti-imperialistic" traditions.

The frustrations and disappointments of an era of the cold war, and the possibility of nuclear wars, are the fate of all mankind. But America has a particular reason for disappointment. For we have been vaulted into a position of world leadership in an incredibly short time. We have renounced the isolationist nationalism, with which we flirted between the two wars, because we neither knew the degree of our power nor were conscious of the responsibilities which are the concomitants of power.

Now we have assumed our world-wide responsibilities with tolerable grace and wisdom, only to find that we are more impotent to master our destiny in the day of our seeming omnipotence than we were in the day of our weakness. The intricate patterns of world history have grown more rapidly than even our rapidly growing power. The natural reaction to such disappointments and frustrations would be vexation and hysteria. But on the political level we have done fairly well in adjusting ourselves to the problems and perils of the new situation. Eisenhower is the agent and the symbol of the acceptance by the business community of the tasks befitting a world power, which the previous isolationism and nationalism tried to disavow. The period of hysteria, for which the late Senator McCarthy was the symbol, was mercifully brief and not as indicative of the American spirit as our foreign detractors, particularly in France, believed or pretended to believe. Politically, our reactions have been fairly wholesome and creative.

But behind the political reactions of our nation are the deeper spiritual reactions of our culture. How adequately have we adjusted ourselves to the total reversal, not only of American, but of our human prospects? The answer to this question must include both the secular and the religious parts of our culture into which the whole of Western civilization has become divided since the Reformation and Renaissance, or more exactly since the seventeenth century.

There are some curious ironies in the reaction of the two portions, which are not, incidentally, as distinct in America as in Western Europe. For in our nation secular and religious viewpoints tend to merge into a kind of vague and sometimes sentimental religion of democracy, with no strong anti-religious or anti-secular fanaticisms. The paradoxical reactions are disturbing at least to Christians, such as the present writer, who regard the so-called revival of religion as rather naive and simple.

This judgement must be clarified and justified by a brief review of our cultural history. Until the present century, the so-called "secularism" against which the religious communities inveighed, as the source of all evil, was in fact not consistently secular. It was religious in the sense that it provided a sense of the ultimate meaning of existence. Its God was "history" or "reason" or "progress" through reason or the advance of the scientific method, or through the application of the methods of science to problems of history. The extravagant hopes of the eighteenth and nineteenth centuries, looking toward the "parliament of mankind and the federation of the world" and promising that history would solve all the problems of the human spirit, certainly aggravated the spiritual crisis of our age. For we know by present experience that historical development enlarges our problems instead of solving them. The United Nations was hardly the "parliament of mankind"; and nothing in the hopes of the previous centuries anticipated the cold war and the precarious nuclear stalemate. Nor did our fathers understand the quality of historical development, which made for progress in the art of war from bows and arrows to guided missiles.

In short, the secularism of previous centuries was incurably utopian. It had renounced the incredible heaven of Plato and the Bible for a more incredible heaven on earth. The utopianism of the liberal nations of Western Europe took many forms; but chiefly the two forms, one of which was symbolized by Herbert Spencer's conviction that history was an extension of nature and that the evolutionary process would guarantee historical progress, if only men would not interfere with the process. The other form of utopianism, symbolized by Auguste Comte, was voluntaristic rather than deterministic and guaranteed progress by the gradual mastery of an elite of scientists over the destinies of men. These utopians were undeterred by the fact that the men, which were to be managed, were possessed of a dignity and recalcitrance which made management difficult; and that even the best scientists were not possessed of the godlike intelligence and distinterestedness which their creed assumed. Western society was saved from the fate of the "Brave New World" described by Aldous Huxley, by the fortunate confusions of democracy, the residual common sense of the common man, and by the failure of the prospective masters of history to plan a political program which would give them the omnipotence which their omniscience would seem to deserve. The soft utopianism of a liberal culture thus proved not incompatible with the preservation of a free society. And the various disciplines of culture enriched the insights and enlarged the competence of the community, even when the specialists were (as was frequently the case) touched with these utopian religions.

Since the facts of history in the early days of industrialism did not at all correspond to these roseate dreams of the soft utopianism, and since the industrial workers were the chief victims of the miscalculations, a new religion of hard utopianism was conceived for them according to which history was moving toward a catastrophic denouement in which the messianic class of the workers, guided by the "vanguard," the party, which alone was privy to the actual "logic of history," would seize control not only of the state, but of history itself. It would make the leap from "the realm of necessity to the realm of freedom," that is, to the freedom to master historical destiny. It was this even more incredible utopianism of Marx, which, frustrated by the common sense of the workers in Western civilization, took root in the decaying monarchial systems of Russia and China, and turned the heaven on earth into a hell by the monopoly of power, with which the Marxist apocalypse endowed the rulers of the utopian theocracy.

No more incredible scheme of salvation was ever offered a credulous people than this secular religion. Its devotees turned out to be, not merely the really desperate poor but the intellectuals of the thirties in Europe and America; and of Asia in the fifties. The fact is mentioned to point to the credulity of the "enlightened" in the so-called secular age.

While history was moving toward the refutation of both

the hard and soft versions of utopianism, the historic forms of faith preserved an unexpected vitality, which the "enlightened" ascribed to the inertia of ignorance and superstition but which was, in fact, partly due to the fact that the mystery of human existence was deeper and higher; the curious combination of the dignity and misery of man (the misery of his sin, guilt and self-contradiction) was more perplexing; his unity as a person in body, mind and spirit was more real; and his uniqueness as an individual was more obvious than was comprehended in any of the religio-scientific analyses of human nature and destiny. Furthermore, history quite obviously moved toward the accentuation of both good and evil, or in biblical symbols, toward the manifestations of Christ and Anti-Christ; and not toward the triumph of good over evil, or of universal over particular community as the utopian creeds anticipated. In short, the historic faiths possessed the dignity of being in touch with mysteries and meanings which were not dreamed of in modern philosophies. They had sufficient dignity, so that they could even survive the obscurantism into which religion is betrayed by regarding its myths and symbols as actual history. These symbols reveal and indicate a depth and height of history. This symbolic task compensates for their lack of scientific exactness.

So matters stood when the frustrations of the twentieth century overtook us. No doubt the refutations of the secular utopian faiths made our generation much more open to the appeal to the traditional historic religions. That is, broadly speaking, the cause for the "revival of religion." But any member of an historic church who is not deluded by the notion that all religion must be good and all secularism bad, is bound to be embarrassed by the fact that the same frustrating experiences, which have sobered secular idealism and divested it of its utopian illusions, seem to have prompted popular support for the most naive and incredible forms of historic faiths. No doubt many Christian pastors and laymen preach and live the message of the gospel in such a way that it will generate charity rather than fanaticism, will persuade men to come to terms with the fragmentariness of all human virtues, the insecurity of all human masteries and to submit all human ambitions and ends to a more total frame of meaning in which the Divine judge corrects and amends the foibles and vanities of men.

But let us look briefly at those forms of modern faith which have particularly caught the public eye. On the West coast, in Los Angeles, the most popular preacher is chiefly intent to equate the freedom of religion with free enterprise; and he defines free enterprise so anachronistically that only an "old," and not a "new," Republican could possibly accept the definition. In any case, religion overwhelms the discriminate judgements upon which justice, particularly in a technical society, depends.

The most popular minister on the East coast is intent upon the identification of faith with the same type of uncritical conservative liberalism; but his chief ambition is to prove that prayer can harness divine power to human ends, particularly to the ends of business success and happiness.

It may come as a surprise to the enlightened critics of the famed evangelist, Billy Graham, that his message is, despite its obscurantist framework ("The Bible says . . ."), or probably because of it, infinitely superior to the other popular versions of the Christian, or at least the Protestant, message. Graham has preserved something of the biblical sense of a

Divine judgement and mercy before which all human strivings and ambitions are convicted of guilt and reduced to their proper proportions. Nevertheless, Graham, under official joint Protestant auspices, presents a simple pietistic version of the Protestant faith which grew on our frontier and which knows nothing of the agonies about the unrighteousness of the righteous out of which the classical Reformation sprang. For according to this pietism, Christians are not completely good and unambiguously virtuous because they have not been properly converted. They have not "accepted Christ," and the "old self" has not been radically destroyed so that the "new self" might emerge. In the old revival meetings, this miracle was performed under the accompaniment of a good deal of emotional agony. But the new evangelism has a blandness which befits the Eisenhower era. The miracle is accomplished by signing a decision card while the choir sings softly. It is a thankless task to criticize Graham, for he is such an honest and sincere, rhetorically skilled protagonist of this faith; and moreover, he is such a photogenic exemplar of Christian virtue that he would feign persuade even the partly sophisticated that he offers at least the basis of the answers to the perplexing problems of nuclear bombs, integration of the schools, child delinquency, and every manner of evil. Undoubtedly, he genuinely helps those who are engulfed in personal moral confusion or in the sense of the meaninglessness of their existence. But Christians will have to agree with responsible and discriminating secularists that the presentation of such a simple version of the Christian faith as an alternative to the discredited utopian illusions is very ironic. It gives even simpler answers to insoluble problems than they. It cuts through all the hard antinomies of life and history by the simple promise that really good people will really be good. It does this at the precise moment when secularism, purged of its illusions, is modestly ready to work at tasks for which there are no immediate rewards and to undertake burdens for which there can be no promise of relief. It has accepted the fact that "sufficient unto the day are the evils thereof" and the tasks thereof.

At any rate, the reactions of our nation to our predicament would not have been possible if the profoundest insights of all the religious and secular disciplines had not been merged so that we are held to our historic tasks, however baffling, and refrain from seeking refuge in either utopia or heaven though we know that both are more or less adequate symbols for the fact that "man's reach is beyond his grasp" and that his historic destiny remains inconclusive to the end.

If we survey our whole situation we must come to the baffling conclusion that the nation, as nation, has done much better in adjusting itself to the curious irony, that it is frustrated in the day of its seeming omnipotence, than the culture has done in sloughing off the utopia illusions of yesterday and coming in touch with the hard realities of twentieth-century life. The national consciousness must have been informed by some hidden resources of common sense which have been withheld from both the wise and the simple. But in the explicitly religious adjustments to the new situation, the enlightened still persist in discredited hopes of historical progress, while, in fact, they come to terms with the hazards of a nuclear age and contemplate without too much hysteria the prospects of success or failure in countering the pressures of a world-wide tyranny without stumbling into an ultimate war and mutual annihilation.

The Christians on the other hand, whose faith in classical form presents the beauty and terror of life without evasion, and whose Christ is at the same time the symbol of the indeterminate possibilities of good, transcending history, and the symbol of the divine mercy, which knows about the ambiguity of all human virtue, have not done so well. They have reduced this majestic faith to petty proportions. Sometimes it becomes a childish lobbying in the courts of the Almighty for special favors. Sometimes it is used rather transparently as a pious ideological weapon of the interests of class and nation. Sometimes it becomes an easy escape from the vexatious issues of the day. Any uncritical satisfaction in these aspects of the religious revival betrays a childishness which compares unfavorably with the adolescent simplicities of the secular utopians of yesterday.

3

HIGHER EDUCATION IN
AMERICA

A study of higher education must begin with an initial distinction between professional and technical education and general education which prepares for both graduate training and for life, and which is, in America at least, the province of the "liberal arts" colleges. The distinction is particularly important in America, where the liberal arts and the "humanities" are rather more rigorously assigned to the colleges than in European countries.

The professional schools transmit the skills and competencies of the various vocations and professions, and the technical schools transmit the sciences and crafts of the technicians and engineers which proliferate in an advanced technical society. We must limit our present survey to the general education of the colleges and universities, which is designed to broaden, to cultivate and to furnish the mind, to enrich the imagination and to redeem the student from the tyranny of time and place by giving him contact with cultures of other ages and civilizations. It is this broad program of general education which must be under immediate survey, though the ends of such an education are as multiple and various as the culture itself. They are in fact so various that it is difficult to establish any useful criteria of judgement.

Perhaps the most plausible criteria of judgement could be expressed in two questions. 1) Does the liberal arts training transmit all the treasures of culture in general and of the national culture in particular with sufficient sympathy for the values of tradition to prevent a sophisticated revolt of the intellectuals against what is valid in the tradition; does it cultivate sufficient discrimination in estimating the different strands in the tradition; and does it encourage sufficient critical detachment from the unique emphases which the peculiarities of the national experience have created to prevent the culture of the nation from becoming too parochial and too dependent upon the past to be relevant and creative in terms of present responsibilities and emergencies?

2) Does the study of the humanities and the whole educational enterprise give the person sufficient cultural resources and intellectual stamina to guard the integrity of the culture and the independence of the individual against the vulgarities and the conformism which are the perils of technical culture with its mass communications and its tendency to emphasize the quantitative, the immediately useful and the standardized canons of taste?

The first criterion, while seemingly arbitrary, is still too broad to be manageable. I will try to limit it by considering the relation of the educational enterprise to two aspects of our culture, the religious and the political. These aspects have been chosen primarily to accommodate the limited competence of the author.

In judging the educational enterprise from the standpoint of its sympathy for, discrimination of and critical detachment from the tradition of our national culture, we are obviously most concerned with our capacity to judge critically between various strands of our tradition, since we are not in peril of lacking sympathy for the "American way of life." It has indeed become the object of a new religious devotion. If critical detachment is regarded as one of the real prerequisities of a creative educational enterprise, we must place chief emphasis upon the freedom of the colleges from ordinary political and ecclesiastical pressure. It is true that there is some pressure from ecclesiastical sources in small denominational colleges and some political domination in state universities. Instances of political pressure and influence upon Boards of Regents in the recent hysterical period remind us of the urgency of the task of preserving "academic freedom."

And yet, American schools are freer of political and ecclesiastical domination than is sometimes assumed by our foreign critics. Most of the state universities have established a traditional freedom from immediate political domination and most of the so-called denominational schools have outgrown their earlier denominational tutelage and are now governed by independent boards. The European scholar will, of course, be critical of this means of governance in our colleges and universities, which contrasts so markedly with the self-governing British tradition and with the very moderate interference which ministries of culture exhibit in the self-governing senates of scholars on the Continent. Let us admit that our college "Boards of Directors" are an irrelevance in the educational enterprise and are sometimes a danger to academic freedom. In the older colleges they have, however, been a resource of freedom against political domination, and in any case, administrative interference is not the chief cause of an absence of critical detachment in our educational enterprise. Such a lack is usually due, not to outside pressure, but to a want of creative vitality in the school itself. Certainly, implicit conformism is always more dangerous and pervasive than explicit conformity due to the fear of power. This is true at least in democratic nations.

If we seek to estimate the power of discrimination and detachment in relation to our political tradition, we may well begin by defining those aspects of our national experience which tend to give our national culture parochial prejudices which the broader perspectives of academic discipline may possibly correct. Three such aspects of our national experience may be discerned. First, our early security tended to make us irresponsible toward the growing world community and obtuse to the perils which we faced in this community. We were not easily cured of this isolationist nationalism, and the dizzy pace of our rise to hegemony in the free world made it difficult to appropriate the lessons of international interdependence by which we now guide our conduct. While it would be wrong to give the universities credit for teaching lessons which the nation learned only through the bitter experience of two World Wars, it is only fair to point out that our political education in the universities was consistently anti-nationalist and contributed to instructing the growing American giant in his world tasks.

The second unique aspect of our political life is the tendency of our business community to equate the cherished liberties of a democratic society with free enterprise in economic life. In times past government was feared as the very apotheosis of power and the root of all evil. A British anthropologist recently attributed this parochial prejudice to the rejection of the father by the mass of our European immigrants. But in fact, the libertarian creed has a simpler and more plausible explanation. The advancing frontier of the nineteenth century and the constantly expanding economy of the twentieth created a kind of middle-class paradise in which the necessity of controlling the economic process by political authority, in Europe expressed in the aristocratic tradition and the proletarian protest against the injustices of the economic order, was subordinated to the belief of the entrepreneur that the automatic balances of the marketplace provided a sufficient guarantee of justice.

Because of this prejudice, our social standards lagged behind those of Europe by half a century until the pragmatic revolutionary movement of the Roosevelt era brought us up to date. Our institutions of higher learning were directly involved in this revolution, in that they furnished the "brain trusters" of Roosevelt's regime and laid the foundation for that curious alliance of farmers, workers, minority groups and intellectuals which has since been the basis of the Democratic Party.

The effect upon the student generation was not so direct. University education seemed to have little influence upon the great majority of university graduates, who continued to be conservative. It would be captious to criticize the schools of learning for not seriously affecting the political opinions of the privileged classes of the community. Such a criticism would assume that the learning process is powerful enough to negate the forces of economic interest. It is important, however, to scrutinize the effect of learning upon the politically sensitive minority of students who, during the depression, not only revolted against the conservatism of their fathers but were inclined to express their revolt by embracing the Marxist creed and in some instances by becoming involved in the Communist conspiracy.

The most fervid American conservatives argue that these youths were beguiled by the Marxism of their teachers. Actually, American universities had little Marxism in their political orientation, perhaps not enough to leaven the lump of conservatism. The social and political thought of the universities was inclined to an uncritical voluntarism, which assumed that the forces of history were manageable by "science" or by "reason" or by the wisdom of man. As a result of this, the intellectual classes were inclined to a soft utopianism, which may have prepared the ground for the hard utopianism of communism. In any case, American intellectuals, like the intellectuals of Asia today, have often been inclined to offer abstract political notions and solutions for complex political problems. This tendency can be contrasted with the commonsense wisdom of the workers, who are intent upon proximate rather than ultimate goals of justice and who, therefore, conform their theories and practices to the truth that men are not only the creators but the creatures of the historical and political process. As creatures they must be more modest and seek to beguile and deflect the historical forces which cannot be as directly managed and whose consequences cannot be as confidently foreseen as the more ambitious managers of historical destiny imagine. It may be relevant to observe that our political life has, since our birth as a nation, been under *both* French and British influences, and that the schools of learning were more prone to the influence of the French Enlightenment than to the more modest and genuinely empirical approach of the British political tradition. Thus political education in America did not make as unambiguous a contribution to the pragmatism of the Rooseveltian revolution as it might have.

The third unique tendency of American political life is the equalitarianism of our political ethos, which undoubtedly derived from the openness of our society and the flexibility of our class structure. Our equalitarianism was not the creed of a resentful, frustrated proletariat but the ethos of a middle-class nation, in which every family had hopes that it could improve its social position, if not in one generation then at least in two or three. Since equality, with liberty, is one of the twin pillars of a free society, there was little reason to expect a critical detachment by the colleges in connection with this aspect of our culture. One may still be critical of the institutions of higher learning for failing to resist a purely quantitative approach to the ideal of equality which would have guarded an aristocracy of excellence against the pressure of mere numbers. Entrance requirements were never made rigorous enough to prevent the inundation of the colleges by students who were not interested in learning but whose parents were interested in using education to signify their own standard of life.

If we turn from the political to the religious traditions of our culture and seek to measure the effect of higher learning upon these traditions, we encounter some difficulty in making any judgements about the relation of the educational enterprise to the religious life of the nation. American religious life is radically unique in the heterogeneity of its religious traditions and in the absolute separation of church and state. Yet there is a greater distance between the secular and the religious community in Europe than among us. Our culture baffles the foreign observer because it is at once more religious and more secular than any other national culture. It is more secular in its frank pursuit of the proximate ends and immediate goals of life; it is more religious in the devotion of a greater percentage of the population to the religious institutions which, contrary to expectation, grow, rather than wither, in the increasingly urban conditions of our technical society. In America religious institutions now claim the allegiance of sixty per cent of the population. The proportion has constantly risen in the last decades and is certainly much greater than in any other "modern" nation.

But the religious institutions to which the majority owe allegiance are less conscious of their relation to an historic church than are the European churches. The various Protestant churches and the Jewish synagogue play a large and creative role in American religious life. One reason for the popularity of the church is that the exclusive sectarian churches on the one hand, and the immigrant churches on the other, have succeeded in establishing integral communities which have made the anonymity of our increasingly urban civilization more tolerable. This is scarcely a religious reason for the popularity of religious institutions, but it may be indirectly related to religious faith, which, whatever its cultural defects, has a frame of reference in which persons are significant. The frame of reference for a consistent rationalism, of whatever type, is bound to depreciate the person in the same way that the applied rationalism of a technical community tends to subordinate the person to social process.

All this religious achievement, probably deficient because

it represents breadth rather than depth, has been accomplished without the benefit of religious teaching in either the lower or higher schools. There is no religious instruction in the public schools and it is forbidden by law in the state universities. Many of the smaller colleges are under the auspices of religious denominations and the old, established, privately endowed universities of the East, which are the main strength of the humanistic tradition, originally were, although they are not now, under religious auspices. They often have departments of religion in which the student may come in contact with both the scriptural historic roots of his faith, and almost all have rather vital extra-curricular religious activities.

We do not, therefore, give a consistently secular education, though the rigorous separation of church and state has certainly affected our culture in many respects. Chiefly it has reduced the religious tradition to a quasi-secular affirmation of those parts of the Christian tradition in which the religious and the secular part of the culture agree. The chief agreement is found in the emphasis on the "dignity of man." The dominant naturalistic mood of our American secularism would seem to be incompatible with this affirmation, but American naturalism is quite able to comprehend or to include all the mysteries of human selfhood in what it calls "nature." Christianity, on the other hand, is inclined to forget or to obscure that the Christian faith speaks both of the dignity and the misery of man; and that its tradition at its best believes both creativity and destructiveness are to be found in man, derived from the same dimension of radical freedom in the human spirit. This virtual agreement between the religious and secular traditions in a common humanism and humanitarianism has prevented the generation of fiercely anti-religious and anti-secular movements. But the price of the accommodation has been that the culture is steeped in a common sentimentality, which, in the period between the two World Wars, influenced the mind of the nation and prevented it from coming to terms with political responsibilities in a world threatened by two forms of tyranny.

There was little difference between the religious and the secular versions of modern utopianism. Both were informed by a common interpretation of human nature, which failed to see the darker side of human conduct and of historical possibilities, being persuaded that men would espouse the common good if only their minds were enlightened by education or their hearts warmed by a vital piety. The secular portion of the culture took these perfectionist ideas from the Enlightenment's conception of human perfectibility, and the church inherited the same optimism from the sectarian perfectionist notions which grew on the frontier. Thus evangelical piety and rational enlightenment combined to give American life a curious air of unreality; they failed to prepare the country for wrestling with problems of domestic justice in a technical age and problems of international justice in an age of tyranny.

The institutions of higher learning did not contribute as much as the common sense of the man in the street (as he appropriated the tragic experiences of our age) to changing the mind and the mood of the nation. They were not, however, involved in the subsequent growth of religious sentimentality, which accompanied the political complacency of the culture, once they had weathered the worst storms of the first half of the century and tried vainly to find peace in an anxious age. Certainly the churches were more involved in this new complacency than the universities, for the piety of the nation was soft while the intelligence of the schools became shrewder and sharper.

This survey of the influence of higher education on the political and religious ideas and the moods of our culture must lead to the conclusion that the universities have been moderately successful in transmitting the treasures of our political and spiritual history and have not been conspicuously successful nor obviously weak in transmitting and adjusting the traditions of our life to the new problems of our age.

II

If the first criterion by which we sought to measure the relation of higher education to our culture seemed arbitrary, our second criterion will probably seem no less so. The criterion is the effectiveness of study in the humanities for guarding the cultural treasures and keeping alive an appreciation of forms of art and science, of imagination and comprehension of life's dimensions, which do not commend themselves in terms of immediate utility and which do not promise an immediate increment of obvious success. This criterion becomes particularly important in a culture which is as preoccupied with technics as is our own. For a technical or technocratic culture generates powerful utilitarian pressures and develops means of mass communication—movies, picture magazines, tabloids, radio and television—which all tend to reduce the culture to a kind of sophisticated vulgarity beside which the vulgarity of the unlettered man of other ages will appear as pure innocence.

The perils of a technocratic culture for the vitality of a humane culture can, of course, be overestimated. It would be

34

unfair to point to the tendency of mass communications to destroy the specialized audiences of special competence, experience and sensitivity, which all the finer arts require for their maintenance, without conceding that the same mass communications have also served to raise the general standards of art and lifted the level of culture from "low-brow" to "middle-brow" levels. It would be fair to say that a technocratic civilization endangers a culture more by its utilitarian pressures than by the vulgarities of its mass communications. The failure of our American culture to reach a high degree of maturity and sophistication, probably because of the utilitarian pressures, is particularly apparent because our commitment to education is so impressive both in the number of years devoted to higher learning and to the number of youths engaged in it.

President Conant has called attention to the uniqueness of our "liberal arts" colleges, which have no counterpart in Europe. In all Western nations, students matriculate directly from high schools, lycées and gymnasia to graduate and professional schools. We insert four years of general education in a college before the student enters a graduate or professional school. If we grant that the European high schools are superior to our own and that the superiority can be quantitatively estimated as the equivalent of two years of study, we would still have a quantitative superiority of two years in the general education of American youths. But quantity is not easily transmuted into quality; that is proved by our general cultural immaturity.

The most obvious defect in the study of the humanities in America is apparent in language studies. Languages succinctly embody the ethos of a culture, so that both modern and ancient languages are the tools and the foundation for the study of the humanities. Yet we are consistently deficient in language studies. Our graduate schools fortunately continue to insist on language requirements for their advanced degrees. But usually the average graduate student masters the languages only in time to pass the examinations and not in time to use them as tools in his preparatory studies.

The colleges may not be primarily responsible for these language deficiencies. The students come to college poorly prepared in language studies because both they and the high-school boards are indifferent to studies which offer no enticements of spontaneous interest or immediate reward. Our American culture is too intent upon the immediate to cultivate those resources of the educational enterprise which require patience and which defer hopes for the sake of some long-range achievement or some competence which can gain only limited popular acclaim.

Our deficiency in language studies is the most obvious and most measurable of the consequences of the utilitarian pressures in our culture. But there are certainly others. The importance of the natural sciences in a nuclear age, and particularly in the "arms race" in nuclear weapons, places a tremendous immediate pressure upon the new generation to devote itself to the natural and the applied sciences. The pragmatic and immediate pressure is so great that the natural sciences are in danger of losing their place as an integral part of the humanities, designed to cultivate the mind of the student, and of becoming merely a preparation for the cultivation of the applied sciences.

The integrity of humanistic studies is also challenged by the increased emphasis upon quantitative measurements in our social studies. Quantitative analyses of various social situations, requiring teams of pollsters rather than the perspective which historical disciplines and imagination supply, have great scientific prestige and are, therefore, popular among the Foundations, who are intent upon advancing the cause of science. They are inclined to regard precise measurement as more scientific than an historical analysis of complex social attitudes and trends. Thus the effort to reduce the social and "behavioral" sciences to the dimension of the natural sciences sacrifices imagination to exactitude. The general effect is to rob the study of the humanities of a dimension of historical empiricism found only in the historical sciences, which tends to impoverish further the genuine humanness of our technocratic culture.

It is difficult to determine whether any defects in the educational process, due to the immediate pressures from the culture or the pressures within the culture itself, are responsible for the general mood of soft conformism into which we have fallen. This conformism is no longer chiefly political nor inspired by the fear of communism and preoccupation with the Cold War. It is broader than any political mood. It is a cultural conformism, partly due to the standardization of tastes through the means of mass communications and partly due to the readiness of ambitious young men to conform their opinions, and even their romantic and family arrangements, to the standards of the big corporations in which they seek employment after graduation.

Either efficiency or success or both have become our supreme end; in this preoccupation there is little scope for the cultivation of a special talent or the pursuit of a non-utilitarian end, and there is little encouragement for the expression of a strange opinion. Our society is too thoroughly integrated to allow the individual to sink, but the forms of integration are so technical that genuine community is frequently unattainable. Paradoxically, the individual develops and is acknowledged only in a genuine community, that is, in a community which is sufficiently non-technical to offer the individual both social fulfillment and the recognition of his uniqueness, together with an appreciation of his desires, hopes and ambitions. The things which are not immediately useful to the community are the very source of the richness and variety of the cultural life of the community.

No educational enterprise can completely free itself of the dominant forces of culture. But it is fair to ask whether there has been a sufficient conscious resistance in the universities to the perils of standardization and conformism in a technocratic society; or a sufficiently patient and resolute determination to guard the long-range ends of humanistic learning against the short-range pressures of a business civilization; or a sufficient imagination in preserving the richness and variety, the breadth and depth of the arts, against the vulgarities of mass communications.

4

RUSSIA AND AMERICA

A Study in Historical Contingency

We must discern the patterns and recurrences of history if we would apprehend some meaning in the phantasmagoria of its expected and unexpected events. We must also find some "moral" meaning, some valid distinction between "good" and "evil" if we want to preserve our moral integrity, or at least sanity, in the multifarious conflicts on the historical scene. But whatever our philosophies and systems of morality, we are inclined to give history a too simple meaning, to press upon its contingent events a too simple logic and to make too simple distinctions between "good" and "evil" which do not conform to the complexity of the configurations and concretions of history in which we try to orient ourselves.

Consider the destiny of the two great nations, Russia and America, which now so unexpectedly dominate the history of mankind, as a case in point. Both nations have a power over the common affairs of the nations which no one could foresee only a half century ago. One especially prescient historian, Alexis de Toqueville, did in fact prophesy something of their present eminence a century ago. But the actual developments were due to so many contingent elements that no one, including de Toqueville, foresaw that Russia would be the holy land of a new political utopian religion or that America would be the champion of "freedom" against the tyranny which developed out of the utopian illusions, or that America would pit its semi-Messianism against the total Messianism of Russia even while it was engaged in providing the highest standards of living for its citizens which any portion of mankind had ever enjoyed. If Russia compounded power impulses with utopian pretensions, America combined preoccupation with comforts and gadgets with a holy zeal against "totalitarianism."

Each of these giants reached its present eminence by a more devious historical route than is immediately apparent and the moral realities are not as simple as each giant imagines, even though the American giant may take satisfaction in having achieved a sense of responsibility toward a total civilization, the "free world," in contrast to the irresponsibility which characterized its life only a half century ago. We are so much more "moral" than anyone had a right to expect in the days of our irresponsibility; and yet so much less moral in the eyes of Asia than we are in our own eyes, that the simple categories which our Secretary of State uses to describe our situation, drawing a distinction between the nations which observe the "moral law" and those which do not, are a source of confusion for the conscience and a hazard to the political prudence which is necessary for our survival.

So many contingent elements have entered into the achievement of the present eminence of the two nations, and so many qualifying factors confuse the distinction between the two as respectively the proponent of tyranny and of freedom, that we must shun all neat attempts at discerning hostorical "logic" or simple efforts to describe the moral distinction between the two giants.

If we consider the contingent elements in the history of both nations we need only to recall that at the beginning of the century or more exactly at the beginning of the First World War in 1914, neither of the nations gave promise of the position which it now holds. Russia was an absolute autocracy which had escaped the leavening influence of both the Reformation and the Renaissance, which helped to form the culture and the political realities of the West. Its anachronistic political system was so little prepared for the dynamics of an industrial civilization which had a bare beginning in her life, that the exertions of a war with a competent and highly industrialized nation created an almost complete collapse of the whole political structure.

Our own nation, on the other hand, was still rocked in the cradle of continental security so that the thunder and alarms of the first great war seemed to it a distant and irrelevant sign of political tumult, from which we were happily spared, because we enjoyed not only an island security but we were, in the words of some of our politicians, happily emancipated from the "tribal conflicts" of Europe.

We were, as we still are, the great bourgeois paradise of the world. We had workers but no proletarians, farmers but no peasants, plutocratic entrepreneurs but no aristocrats. We indulged in an extravagant individualism which would have ruined any European nation, but which the expanding frontier and our subsequent expansion of industry and trade, seemed to make morally and politically viable. We had no static "classes" and therefore no class resentments. We had little sense of the contrivances which were needed to make liberty compatible with justice and stability; and we certainly had little conception of belonging to a Western European civilization or of our growing power in the community of nations or of the responsibilities of that power.

We were on the way of becoming the most technocratic, mechanized and urban of all Western cultures, but the myths of an agrarian democracy, initiated by Jefferson, still dominated our political thought. We thought that democracy meant a minimal restraint upon every man seeking by diligence and thrift to advance the fortunes of his family. The independent man of the soil, mixing his labor with a generous nature, was our ideal long after the urban population had supplanted the farmer in power and prestige.

If Russia was drawn into the First World War beyond the competence of her power, we were drawn into it beyond our understanding or conscious intent. We did not know that our security was parasitic on British power, particularly sea power, though our final and reluctant participation in the war, allegedly prompted by abhorrence of the Germans' method of warfare particularly on the seas, was probably actually motivated by an only partly conscious realization that the Germans were about to upset the power balances upon which our security depended. We were certainly not conscious of the imminent fate awaiting us: that we were about to supplant Britain as the hegemonous power in the Western world. We were undoubtedly drawn into the war by impulses deeper than conscious knowledge and more potent than the conscious reasons which we gave for our actions. The fact that we did not quite understand what we were doing is proved by our subsequent conviction that our involvement in European wars was a mistake, that it was due to an inadvertence, and that future entanglements could be avoided by rigorous neutrality laws. A Senate investigation committee solemnly tried to prove that bankers and munition makers were responsible for our involvement, and in fact, for wars in general. Thus, only a little before we were called upon to assume the trying responsibilities of an hegemonous power in a dramatic struggle between democracy and tyranny, we gave ourselves to the childish delusions of conspirational interpretations of world politics. We were suddenly promoted from childhood to an uneasy maturity by the same historical forces which completely destroyed an old Russian autocracy and put in its place a dynamic autocracy, dedicated, not to the status quo but to world revolution.

The First World War thus destroyed the old Russia and rocked the cradle of the American infant giant. All subsequent happenings in the lives of both nations were the elaborations of hidden potentialities, which men could have known had they been more observant, and of historical contingencies which men could not foresee. The breakdown of Czarism was expected to yield a belated democratic revolution after the Western pattern. But the Kerensky régime did not last long partly because of the ineptitude of its leaders, but mainly because the middle classes of industrial society, which were the natural bearers of such a revolution, had not reached the strength which they possessed in the West. The communist revolution throttled the democratic revolution. The communist revolution—where did that come from? The revolution which overturned Russia and changed the whole course of modern history was designed by Karl Marx as the final climax of judgement and redemption for advanced capitalistic societies. According to Marx's prophecies, America would have been the ideal ground for such a revolution. Instead, the revolution occurred in Russia. This revolution was "inevitable" in the sense that the old dynastic structure of Russian society collapsed so completely, and that the possibility of a middle-class democratic revolution was so remote, that the communist revolution would seem to have been the only alternative.

Yet, many contingent developments of history entered into the formation of this alternative. We have been so long in an attitude of polemical tension with communism that we have not had the inclination to understand it as a very curious and unexpected historical phenomenon. Marxism is a secularized version of Christian-sectarian apocalypse which expresses a perennial hope of mankind to break through the perennial ambiguities of history and establish a kingdom of perfect brotherhood on earth. The sectarian Christians of Cromwell's army in the seventeenth century with their hope of establishing the "Fifth Monarchy," that of Jesus Christ, after the destruction of the "fourth monarchy" of Charles I, set the pattern for this sort of modern religious apocalypse. Marx elaborated these apocalyptic hopes with a dash of Hegelian "dialectic" and one of French materialism. He presented, in short, a materialistic version of historical dialectic according to which the "class struggles" of history would inevitably work toward a climax of injustice in modern capitalism. In this climax, the very ambiguity of history would be resolved; and the revolutionists, by taking timely action in the hour of crisis, would not only destroy capitalism as a system of production but they would translate the whole of humanity from the "kingdom of necessity to the kingdom of freedom." The point is that men would be emancipated from the curious ambiguity of being at once creators and creatures of the historical process and would become absolute masters of their own destiny. This was obviously not simply an economic and social theory but a scheme of redemption. It was the more plausible because it confronted a secular age as a "science." Had not Marx's *Das Kapital* proved scientifically that history was in the process of moving "dialectically" to this climax of judgement and redemption? Historical developments made it inevitable that the rich would become richer and fewer and the poor would become poorer and more numerous until it would be a simple matter for the poor to make this great change in the human situation driven by the desperation of their poverty. They would be the "midwife" of the new order. They were the Messianic class. There were some difficulties in casting the industrial poor (and only the industrial poor were envisaged in Marx's apocalypse) for this role. For the poor might have the revolutionary resentment to take drastic action, but they did not know the logic of history which had marked them out as the redeemers of mankind. Only the communists knew this logic and they would therefore act as the "vanguard of the proletariate" and tell the poor what they really wanted and what they really desired, if they only knew the logic of history well enough. Thus, the germ of changing the "dictatorship of the proletariate" into the dictatorship of a political party was in the Marxist apocalypse.

How did this strange religion of redemption, posing as a science, gain a foothold in either Europe or Asia? The answer is that it first gained a foothold in the European civilization for which it was designed, because the social facts of early European industrialism seemed to make its implausibilities plausible. The "bourgeoisie," the "ruling classes," did seem to make political power subservient to their greed; there seemed to be no effective check upon their power; and economic power seemed to be more primary than political power, though ultimately the communist tyranny refuted the idea of the primacy of economic power and proved that political power is always primary. It must be added that the Marxist apocalypse seemed particularly plausible if capitalistic economics were superimposed upon a feudal class structure. Only in that way would there be sufficient "class consciousness" and class resentments to fit the Marxist scheme. The absence of the feudal class system in America prevented Marxism from becoming a living creed here despite the injustices of early industrialism. Even in Europe democratic political power was much more potent and the flexibilities of a democratic society were much more fruitful in establishing those equilibria of power in both the economic and political sphere upon which justice depends. Marxism, therefore, though it became the working creed of European industrial classes, lacked historical dynamic. The desperation which Marx anticipated did not develop except in a few nations after the First World War. And even in such cases the deterministic elements in Marxism tended to prompt an attitude of "watchful waiting" among the allegedly desperate working classes for the revolutionary crisis. Furthermore, a class struggle which Marx did not anticipate developed among the working classes themselves. Only the most desperate workers, the unemployed and the unskilled, adopted the orthodox Marxist revolutionary creed. The less resentful, because more secure, workers elaborated various democratic versions of Marxism. In short, the plausibility of the Marxist scheme of redemption was very short-lived in the

46

civilization for which it was intended. It had only sufficient plausibility to attract the intellectuals and the most desperate workers. It still attracts them both in such nations as France, with its moribund capitalism, and Italy, with its semi-feudalism.

It was this scheme of salvation, implausible in a technical and democratic society, which found lodgement in Russia after the breakdown of the old monarchial system.

One might argue that a decaying feudal order produces more revolutionary resentments than the open society of a technical civilization; and that therefore this jump from capitalism to feudalism of the Marxist creed is logical or "inevitable" enough. But the jump could not have occurred without the highly contingent leadership of a Marxist revolutionary by the name of Lenin.

Lenin is one of those figures in history whose "contingent" emergence in the historical scheme makes nonsense of any philosophy of history which relies upon the alleged discernment of "patterns" and "objective forces" as the clues to historical development. Trotsky, in his *History of the Russian Revolution,* has difficulty in placing Lenin in the framework of his deterministic creed. He finally settles for the idea that "great men" can hasten the fulfillment of the "logic" of historical development. As a matter of fact, Lenin did more than hasten the fulfillment. Without his unique gifts the revolution in Russia would not have been possible.

Lenin's chief revolutionary gift was an absolute fanaticism, combined with tactical flexibility. His absolute fanaticism made it possible to organize a close-knit party, which allowed no cooperation with even the most revolutionary political parties, and discouraged "factions" within the communist

47

party itself. He thus built a compact political power with a strong sense of direction in a situation where every other political force was confused and without a sense of direction. Lenin, secondly, increased the proportion of voluntarism in what was hitherto a delicate balance of determinism and voluntarism in the Marxist creed. The true believer would have to wait for the logic of history to move toward the final climax. It was only then that he must act as a "midwife" of the new order. Actually, since the anticipated climax would never correspond to actual historical facts, the truly orthodox believer was bound to upset the balance by waiting for something which would never happen. Lenin emphasized the necessity of hastening the climax by action. The communists became the voluntaristic sect of the Marxist orthodoxy, both in Europe and in Asia.

But something more than emphasis on action was needed in an agrarian feudalism involved in catastrophic dissolution. This catastrophe was totally different from the anticipated catastrophe of an over-ripe capitalism. The industrial poor, marked by the apocalypse as the redeemers of mankind, were in a small minority in a community in which industrialism had barely begun. The masses of disaffected and resentful poor were soldiers and peasants, or rather, soldier peasants, suffering from the breakdown of both the military and the political order. They were not interested in the collectivism, designed for and only relevant to industrial workers. Lenin designed a revolutionary slogan for them which was not in the original Marxist orthodoxy. It was "land, peace and bread." It has since been the unvarying policy of "Leninism" to promise poor peasants land in order to enlist them in the revolutionary camp and then take the land away from them and "collectivize" it, once the party is in full control of the situation. The peasants' love of the soil has, incidentally, forced them into fascist camps in opposition to a collectivist program, so heedless of his particular view of "property" in every situation in which absolute breakdown has not occurred so quickly as to deprive the peasant of all instruments of power.

At any rate, the peasant was provisionally enrolled in the army of revolution. Subsequently, millions of peasants were starved and liquidated in the forced collectivization program under Stalin. The fact that the Chinese dictator, Mao, who originally had a more moderate program for the peasants, has recently embarked upon forced collectivization, seems to prove that the logic of communism demands this step, both because it is necessary to make all classes powerless in a dictatorship and because it is necessary to transmute the peasants into something resembling the industrial proletariate who are, after all, the destined Messianic class in the original orthodoxy.

One interesting contingent factor must be mentioned additionally. Lenin had promised "peace" as well as land and bread. How was he going to fulfill that promise when the German armies were still intact and the Germans intent on devouring as much of the Russian Empire as possible? Lenin solved that problem by a miscalculation based upon the Marxist dogma. He submitted to the exorbitant demands of the Germans at Brest-Litovsk and the peace was signed. But even Lenin's immense authority would not have persuaded even the communist party to yield to these demands, if it had not been believed that a revolution would soon break out in Germany and would rectify this draconic peace. Thus, an error rooted in the Marxist dogma had to come to the aid of the unscrupulous genius of Lenin before the communists could hold all the levers of power in their hands, making Russia the holy land of the new political religion which was to engulf almost the whole of Asia and substituting a dynamic tyranny dedicated to revolutionary change, for the static tyranny of the Czars, committed to the status quo. The fact that there was no intervening freedom or democracy helped to make the tyranny sufferable. We need not follow the course of that tyranny too carefully for the main outlines of its history are well known. As Stalin succeeded Lenin, the "democratic centralism" gave way to pure tyranny, not as Khrushchev would now have it, by the contingent lust for power of one man, but as the result of what the Marxists define as "objective conditions." Those factors were the monoply of power established in the name of the Marxist dictatorship of the proletariate by the party. The freedom in the community outside the party having been destroyed, it was easy for the oligarchy within the party to destroy the freedom of the members of the party; and subsequently for a single dictator to destroy the freedom of the oligarchy. It is this latter development which the present leadership is so anxious to cancel; without, however, destroying the oligarchic power of the "collective leadership."

Many contingent factors undoubtedly contributed to the triumph of communism in Russia. But once it had become established, many of the developments of communism both in Russia and in the world proceeded by "logical" necessity. They were logical in the sense that given the establishment of a secular utopian political religion claiming a single nation as its "holy land," it was inevitable that its prophets should turn into priest kings and that it should appeal to that part of the world in which political and social conditions were similar to those of Russia. It was inevitable, in short, that a creed which was not plausible for the civilization for which it was designed should be plausible for the nations of Asia and Africa.

These nations were receptive to communism for at least four reasons. 1) They all were agrarian nations with a decadent feudal social order which created more social resentments than the injustices of capitalism because there seemed less hope of correcting them. 2) They had an additional reason for finding communism plausible which the Russians did not have. They were either ex-colonial nations or they had, like China, suffered from the white man's arrogance and from the impact of technically powerful nations upon the technically weak nations. Their experience seemed to validate that part of the Marxist credo which derived "imperialism" from capitalism. Since the Russian will-to-power was more recent and operated chiefly in Europe rather than Asia, it was possible for the new imperialism to obscure its will-to-power and to pose as the champion of the weak. Thus, an improbable Marxist dogma seemed to have gained both relevance and validity. The self-righteousness of the so-called "free" nations, which had forgotten their rather ruthless power politics of the nineteenth century and had only emancipated the colonial nations when the post-war weakness and weariness had made continued rule impossible, contributed to the success of the communist cause in both Asia and Africa. 3) Communism represented an historic dynamism which awakened the sleeping-waking cultures of the Orient, informed either by world-denying mystic faiths or by static forms of humanism, as Chinese Confucianism. The West had profited by the historical dynamism of the Judaeo-Christian religious tradition. This heretical utopian dynamism was the more impressive to the desperate and resentful people of the Orient because its promises were false. They were false in the sense that they promised goals which cannot be reached in history. Utopia seems a plausible goal to the peoples who have never experienced the tortuous processes of history except in terms of expectation. 4) Communism promised Asia and Africa the possibility of technical competence without the hazards of democratic life. None of the newly emancipated nations could be sure that freedom could be made as compatible with both stability and justice as it has in fact proved to be in Western history. But since four centuries were required to prove this compatability and since unique resources of the West, frequently not repeatable in the Orient, entered into the proof of compatibility, the scepticism of the Orient was seemingly justified. In any event, Lenin's definition of communism as "the Soviets plus electricity" was one of the few promises which communism fulfilled. It has become increasingly attractive to the non-European world simply as the bearer of technical competence without the hazards of the delicate equilibria of power by which the Western world maintains both liberty and justice.

Thus, a world-wide political religion has attained tremendous plausibility and power, though it might, in Winston Churchill's phrase, have been "throttled in its cradle" in its infancy and depended upon some vivid historical contingencies for its original success.

Thus, one of the giants of the present historical scene grew to strength by the most improbable historical contingencies which no one could have foreseen and which we cannot completely understand even though we have seen and recorded them.

The other giant, our own nation, had a less improbable development but many historical contingencies entered into our history also before we could bear our present responsibilities in the world community with a tolerable measure of success. It may seem perverse to compare President Franklin D. Roosevelt with Lenin. The one was an absolute revolutionist and the other a democratic statesman who had developed the art of opportunism and pragmatism to such a pitch that he literally beguiled the nation beyond its conscious wisdom, both to assume the responsibilities of its power and to qualify its political individualism, its conservatism composed of a decadent Manchester liberalism, so that a tolerable justice could be achieved within the framework of an ever-growing industrial efficiency and productivity. Until the Rooseveltian revolution, the right of labor to organize and bargain collectively was not universally accepted though it is an indispensable pre-requisite for establishing the equilibrium of power upon which justice depends in a technical civilization. Nor had our type of conservative liberalism regarded it as necessary to use the power of the state to establish minimal securities for the workers exposed to the hazards of collective life, which Bismarck had recognized as a political necessity a half century earlier in Germany. The revolution under Roosevelt, in short, prepared the nation to take its place as an hegemonous power in a democratic world with something more than the preponderance of economic power to give it prestige. The Rooseveltian era hastened our political development so far beyond our conscious political intent, that our business community, reluctantly accepting what had been accomplished in the revolution, still persists in creating an image of ourselves

53

which is ironically similar to the communist caricature of our national life. In each case freedom is emphasized without recognizing that we have made freedom compatible with justice and political stability. Without such compatibility freedom is an irrelevance to nations which are concerned to preserve stability and to gain justice, and who do not know whether or how these ends can be achieved within the frame of a democratic society.

In foreign policy Roosevelt understood better than the "liberal" political forces, which he had organized into a new political power, that it was both in accordance with our national interest and with our professed morality to come to the aid of an imperiled European democracy, suffering under attack from an unscrupulous totalitarianism. American liberalism was informed by pacifistic, moralistic and isolationist illusions, so that the nation was almost as reluctant to engage in its second adventure in world politics as in the first one. Ironically, the conservatives of the type of Henry Stimson and the "international bankers," villains of the myths of the First World War, understood the perils and responsibilities of the nation better than the political forces behind Roosevelt. They contributed greatly to his second election. But even their help would not have served to shock the nation out of its shivering indecision if the Japanese militarists had not catapulted us into the war. Thus, we were shoved into the position, which we now hold, beyond our intent and our wisdom. The Japanese miscalculation must be numbered among those historical contingencies which make nonsense of the neat patterns of history by which we try to understand our collective destiny.

We entered the war, the second, as the first time, belatedly and peripherally. But we emerged from it the undisputed dominant power of the democratic world. Almost miraculously the consciousness of our power and the attendant satisfactions in wielding it, cured us of our irresponsibility. Even while our democratic allies feared a possible return to our immature irresponsibility, we assumed a posture of responsibility, which sometimes frightened our allies by its inflexibility. In fact, a note of hysteria entered into our assumption of power. We had acquired it without consciously striving for it. We had not served an apprenticeship in the manipulation of political forces. We were ostensibly an "anti-imperialistic" nation, called upon to lead a great "empire" of "free" nations. We had achieved this hegemony partly by the great economic power in our possession and partly by the military power which in a technical age is so easily derived from technical power. Meanwhile, military weapons had achieved the lethal proportions of an atomic age.

For these and other reasons, the previous moralism of the nation, which identified neutrality with innocence, was quickly transmuted into an even simpler moralism, which established our virtue by the consistency of our enmity to a hated totalitarian foe, who had been our provisional ally in the defeat of another type of totalitarianism. In these complexities it was natural, but also neurotic, to flee to simple formulae of meaning and morality. We needed these formulae the more because we faced frustrations of our will in the days of our seeming omnipotence which we had not confronted in the days of our weakness and assumed innocence. We could simplify the meaning of our collective destiny by an image of ourselves as the potent protagonist of democratic virtue against the evils of tyranny.

But this simple moral category of meaning is as confusing,

though provisionally justified, as the too-simple concepts of historical logic by which we seek to comprehend the destiny of nations.

But what was the freedom of the "free" world and what was totalitarianism? Ostensibly the meaning of these two categories was simple and the contrast was complete. The free world meant the world in which each nation and individual could fulfill its potentialities with a minimum of coercion, and the totalitarian world was that curious domain in which tyranny had grown on the ground of utopianism.

But many factors qualified this simple contrast. The democratic world boasted of a political freedom which was a necessity of justice. But it had only achieved a tolerable justice very recently, which proved that freedom was compatible with justice only if the various equilibria of power in the political and economic sphere could be established. Political freedom was a necessity, but it was also a luxury which the Western world had required centuries to perfect and to make it compatible with justice. Political freedom was, in short, a luxury which the nascent nations, without the previous history of the Western world might not be able to afford. Perhaps it was a luxury which only nations possessing the flexibilities of a technical civilization and the elbow room of an expanding economy could afford. Perhaps democracy was not only the prerequisite of justice, but the luxury, which only a community untroubled by internal and external dangers could afford.

But the chief reason why the cause of the "free world" did not seem as virtuous as we had assumed, was that the free world was also the white world and the technically competent world, the nineteenth-century impact of which upon the agrarian and technically backward nations of Asia and Africa was "imperialistic." Its power impulses seemed to validate the Marxist indictment of "capitalism" as the real root of imperialism. The white man's arrogance had left the Asian and African world with residual resentments even after the Western nations, weakened by the two wars, had been forced to grant many of the colonial nations their freedom. In the case of the French Empire in Africa, it continued to be a present source of moral odium.

Our own nation, with its ex-colonial past and previous anti-imperialistic convictions, thought it could free itself of this odium; but in politics, particularly international politics, the doctrine of guilt by association is potent, particularly when the allegedly anti-imperialistic nation thinks it can support a discredited Chinese government against the communist power purely by force of arms. One of the ironic developments of recent years is that an ex-imperialist power, Great Britain, is more popular in India than we are. In any case, we are dealing not only with the moral prestige of our nation, but of the whole alliance of free nations, comprising primarily the European nations who boast of domestic democratic achievements but who must all confess an imperialist past, involving more or less creative imperialistic achievements. But these are in any case forgotten in the resentment against past exhibitions of racial arrogance. The democratic world has only recently become fully conscious of the taint upon its virtue, created by past sins. If we are not as unvirtuous as our neutral or communist critics regard us, we are certainly not as pure as the simple moral contrast which we imagine defines the issue between us. The simple fact is that a Western civilization, tainted by previous imperialistic relations to the Asian world, has been called upon to defend both itself and its privileges against the utopian fury of a political religion, with a culture which it is trying to change from its agrarian base to modern industrialism. Some of the evils of Western industrialism appear in a new way in this process. Capital investments must be created by the postponement of present consumption. The utopian politics which promised to make the poor rich, is now forced to postpone the fulfillment of these promises for the sake of ultimate collective wealth. Communism has become to the whole non-technical world, not only the symbol of freedom from foreign oppression, but the hope of technical competence and industrial wealth without the hazards of the instabilities associated with freedom.

The fact that new injustices are inherent in its monopolies of power and that these injustices have already revealed themselves both in the domestic life of nations and in the relations of Russia to the lesser communist nations has been obscured by the force of the utopian creed. The revelations and confessions of the regnant oligarchy in Russia about the shocking injustices of the Stalin regime prompt disillusionment in some quarters, but the hope of a new freedom in others. The whole communist empire is no doubt subject to a leavening process in which the old orthodoxy will be gradually changed. But the history of the Roman autocracies, both West and East, do not prompt optimism about the quick development of freedom, particularly not as a grant from the oligarchs now in power.

The ideological and moral fuzziness around the edges of the simple moral contrast between freedom and absolutism do not change the moral realities and responsibilities which weigh upon the politics of the Western alliance. But they do invalidate the moral complacency which has confused the politics of the West. We cannot survive and a free society cannot evolve in the world which is changing tutelage for independence and agrarianism for industrialism, if our policy is not more fully aware of the historical contingencies which have blurred the too-simple picture of righteousness in conflict with evil, which has both generated our willingness to engage in the struggle and our complacency in analyzing the factors at work in the contest.

Meanwhile, an ironic dimension has been added to the struggle by the development of nuclear weapons, which make mutual annihilation a possibility should the two world forces stumble into an ultimate conflict. Our original monopoly in the weapons of mass destruction has been changed by the fact that the Russians learned the scientific secrets of nuclear development both by stealing them from us and by being much more resourceful technically than we thought they would be.

The resulting stalemate in nuclear weapons has introduced one hopeful element into this world contest. It has prompted both sides both to realize and to admit that the other side is not intent on war. On our part this changes the whole posture of defense against an inevitable catastrophic war, which was prompted by the dubious analogy between the Nazi and the communist tyrannies, and the resultant conviction that the communist system could not gain victories except by military adventures. Meanwhile its philosophy and its successes in the Asian world made it chary of military ventures and hopeful of its prospects of gaining supremacy in the world by political subversion, by diplomatic pressures, by the technical aid of non-technical nations, by every means, in short, which would not risk an ultimate conflict.

In this situation it is obviously necessary to combine our devotion to the cause of democratic freedom with a shrewd understanding of the many contingent and unpredictable elements which have entered into the struggle.

Both the logic and the morality of historical contests are more complex than the contestants are likely to realize. The dramas of history are without dramatic or logical neatness, and the moral issues prove that in history the "wheat and the tares" are really as mingled as the scriptural parable warns. We must make our judgement from day to day. But we should recognize that both political and moral judgements are provisional and tentative. We are creatures as well as creators of history.

5

LIBERTY AND EQUALITY

Insofar as the debate between conservatism and liberalism is a contest between the beneficiaries and the victims of any given status quo, it may be politically potent but it is philosophically uninteresting. It merely reveals the ideological taint in our political preferences. But the debate may mean more than that. It may involve the significance of the two principles of liberty and equality as principles of justice. Traditional conservatism and liberalism have contrasting attitudes toward those principles, conservatism being usually indifferent to them, while liberalism appreciates them as regulative principles and sometimes erroneously regards them as simple historical possibilities.

But even a debate on this level tends to become otiose because the history of the great democratic nations tends to separate truth from falsehood in each political philosophy and to create a legitimate conservatism and legitimate liberalism, which are nearer to each other than either is to a cynical conservatism or to an abstract liberalism. We must try to find the reasons for this development in political thought. They are related on the one hand to the inevitability and on the other hand to the corruption of the social gradations and the non-voluntary forces of social cohesion which enter into every form of stable community.

Every community is organized through a hierarchy of authority and function, and its forces of cohesion contain such non-voluntary and sub-rational forces as kinship feeling, geographic contiguity, common memories and common fears, and ultimately the police power of the state, the community's chief organ of unity and will. The principle of "equality" is a relevant criterion of criticism for the social hierarchy, and the principle of "liberty" serves the same purpose for the community's unity. But neither principle could be wholly nor absolutely applied without destroying the community.

To validate this thesis it will be necessary to analyze in turn the relation of equality to the realities of the social or political hierarchy and the principle of liberty to the realities of communal cohesion and stability. The necessity of a gradation of authority and function in any community or common enterprise must be obvious to even the most casual observer. Every school with more than one room is coordinated under the authority of a "principal"; and every school system with more than one school has a superintendent. Most churches have a hierarchy of superintendents, deacons, or bishops. Communities of common work reveal the same gradations of function and authority. A specialized production operation is governed by a foreman, and the total production is governed and coordinated by a "production manager." The other specialized functions of sales, promotion, and finance each have their managers, or, in this latter day, "vice presidents." The whole enterprise is governed by a president or general manager, who is usually under the authority of a board of trustees, representing the owners, in the modern case usually multiple owners. The managerial oligarchy has proved more important than the original theories of ownership anticipated, but that is another story. The political order is integrated by the same sort of hierarchical structure.

Political communities of early days grew gradually from tribe to city-state and from city-state to empire. The instrument of cohesion in an early empire was usually some dominant city-state, even as the instrument of unity in the city-state was a king, originally a tribal chieftain, or perhaps, as in Greece, the authority was wielded by a whole aristocratic class. The national community was a fairly late development in Western history; its unity was usually the result of ethnic kinship, a common language, and the dominance of the king over the nobles. Democratic institutions were the final but not the first instruments of national unity. Democracy has brought arbitrary power under check and made it responsible, but it has not seriously altered the hierarchical structure of the community. Even democratic communities are integrated by military and civil bureaucracies and by local legislative assemblies and governors. The military order depends upon a rigorous adhesion to the "chain of command."

The distinctions in function invariably involve a distinction of authority for the higher functions, and greater authority means greater power. Prestige or "majesty" is the inevitable concomitant of power, and it in turn becomes the very source of power, insofar as power is usually the ability to win uncoerced consent. Special privilege flows inevitably from the exercise of power. The distinctions of power and prestige are very great in traditional communities because they are necessary to achieve the unity of the community. The majesty of the king is, in fact, usually the symbol and instrument of the majesty of the community. Its inordinant degree is intended to discourage dissent, for traditional communities have not yet found a way of allowing dissent within the framework of unity. But beside this functional necessity of excessive distinctions in prestige there was always the ideological factor that the greater the authority and power of a leader the more does he himself determine the degree of power and prestige which he is to enjoy. One must regard it as axiomatic therefore that gradations of power and prestige were never exactly proportioned to the social function which furnished their basic justification.

Inequalities of privilege were, of course, always partly proportioned to prestige and function. But they never corresponded exactly to these inequalities of function. They exceed the requirements of social function ever more obviously as one ascends the social hierarchy. We thus confront the two basic realities of the community's social hierarchy. The one is that such a hierarchy is necessary, and the other is that the prestige, power and privilege, particularly privilege, of its upper levels tend to be inordinate. That is why there can be no simple solution for the problem of social gradation. That is why equality must remain a regulative principle of justice and why equalitarianism is the ideology of the poor. They resent the inequalities, rightly because of their inordinate character; but they wrongly imagine that all inequalities could be abolished. Inequalities are no doubt more excessive in traditional communities than they are in the modern "liberal" states. They are unduly so partly because the traditional communities, whether in the medieval West or in modern Asia and Africa, needed to pay the price of inordinate gradation of prestige and power for the boon of communal unity, and partly because the communities lacked sufficient equalibria of power to establish equality.

Modern business and industrial civilization were regarded by the strict equalitarians, the Marxists, as tending to accentuate the inequalities of traditional societies; and there were indeed early indications that this would be the case. The business community, on the other hand, whether honestly or ideologically, expressed the hope that political liberty would gradually lead to general equality, in the economic and in the political sphere. This hope was mistaken in the short run but not in the long run. Political liberty did not yield relative equality until the poorer classes achieved both political and trade-union organizations by which they could set organized power against organized power.

This equilibrium of organized power has refuted the catastrophic predictions of Marxism and rendered the Western world safe against revolutionary resentment. But it has not eliminated the necessity of the gradation of function and authority, as presupposed by an abtract equalitarianism. The social hierarchy is as omnipresent in a "liberal" community as in a traditional one, and for that matter in a communist one. Nor has it eliminated excessive privilege for the higher degrees of authority and competence. In fact, a commercial and competitive society adds competition for the highest positions as a further reason for excessive privilege. That is the reason that the great business executives draw salaries greater than the salary of the President of the nation. The corruption of a necessary gradation of authority is as inevitable as the gradation itself, and justifies the criterion of equality as a permanent challenge to the real and potential injustices in the community, and as a way of reducing the excesses by scrutinizing every privilege in relation to the function to which it is attached.

The principle of liberty is related to the unity of a society as the principle of equality is related to the hierarchical structure of the community. It is a twin regulative principle and it is in the same danger of being regarded as a simple historical possibility. The unity and stability of traditional communities, from primitive days to the end of the medieval period in the West, and to the present day in Asia and Africa, were achieved by permitting as little dissent as possible and by enforcing conformity, not chiefly by force and terror, as in the modern totalitarian state, but by a culture-and-custom-enforced idolatrous devotion to the community as the final end of human existence. Every community seeks unity and stability as the price of existence itself, for chaos means non-existence. The long popularity of the dynastic monarchy in the history of nations was due to the efficacy of this institution in assuring a single unchallenged organ of unity to the state and in assuring a method of transmitting authority from generation to generation without exposing the community to the chaos of conflicting choices of authority. The unity of the community seemed to eliminate liberty as a possibility as rigorously as the hierarchical structure seemed to eliminate equality. The unity and stability of the community makes liberty even today less than an absolute right. Nevertheless, the tendency of the community to claim the individual's devotion too absolutely, and to disregard his hopes, fears, and ambitions which are in conflict with, or irrelevant to, the communal end, makes it necessary to challenge the community in the name of liberty.

Liberty is just as unrealizable in the absolute sense and just as relevant as the principle of equality.

According to democratic mythology, particularly in France and America, it was the French Revolution which first introduced these twin principles of liberty and equality to history (together with the ideal of "fraternity" which was at once more relevant and more irrelevant to practical politics). It was certainly the French Enlightenment which nourished the illusion of the historical realizability of the two principles. But they originated in the previous century among the Christian radicals on the left wing of Cromwell's army. The Enlightenment merely provided a secular version of the apocalyptic visions of these Christian sectaries. But one of the two principles had a much longer history than that: "equality." It was first introduced by Greek stoicism as a principle of justice, and strangely enough was popularized by the Roman Stoics, who were politicians and lawyers rather than philosophers, and who insisted on the relevance of the principle despite the hierarchial structure of the Roman imperial state. Aristotle defined justice as the disposition "to give each man his due" and was careful to apportion the "due" of the superior and the inferior man. His political philosophy was influential in sanctifying not only the classical but the medieval aristocratic structure. In contrast, Seneca, who with Cicero may be deemed the father of all modern political sentimentality, thought that free man and slave "were but names springing from ambition and injury." Stoic equalitarianism did not seriously affect the class structure of the Roman state. In fact the Stoic idealists were more realistic than their French inheritors because they relegated the principle of equality to a mythical "golden age," in which the *Jus Naturale* was absolutely applied. In actual history the institutions of slavery, government, and property were observed to be universal restraints enjoined or allowed by the *Jus Gentium,* the law of nations. Thus Stoicism expressed, if not consistently, the idea that equality was a regulative principle of justice but not directly applicable to the life of the community. That insight was superior to the simple equalitarianism of the French Enlightenment.

The classical age did not put the principle of liberty in conjunction with the principle of equality, but neither was it discovered by the French Enlightenment. The English sectaries were the first to join liberty with equality as one of the two principles of justice. The idea of the freedom of the individual did not emerge until it had the support first of the Christian faith, with its high value for the uniqueness of the individual and with its belief that the individual had a source of authority and an ultimate fulfilment transcending the community. But this alone did not establish individual liberty as a principle of justice. If the religious foundation had been all that was necessary to grant the individual freedom from the communal whole, liberty would have been propounded and achieved in the Christian ages of Europe. But Catholic Christianity had its own interpretation of liberty. For it, liberty meant the right of the individual to seek his "eternal" rather than his temporal end, and this end could be guaranteed by the church rather than the political community. Even the Protestant Reformation, which rebelled against the authoritarian church, did little to vindicate the right of the individual against the state. Luther's ideal of "evangelical" liberty was religiously potent but politically irrelevant because it did not challenge the authority of the state over the conscience of the individual. It wasn't until Milton interpreted the well-known words of Scripture "Give unto Caesar the things that are Caesar's and to God the things that are God's" to mean "My conscience I have from God and I can therefore not give it to Caesar" that the religious ideal became relevant to political and civil liberty.

But the rise of the commercial middle class, with its more mobile forms of property and with its desire for individual initiative, was required to break the mold of a purely organic and traditional society and to insist on liberty as a regulative principle of justice. Ever since the seventeenth-century libertarian principles have been motivated by both ultimate and economic motives; and middle-class libertarianism was expressed both in John Stuart Mill's "Essay on Liberty" and Adam Smith's "Wealth of Nations." In the one case the individual was vindicated against the community, and in the other a philosophical basis for "free enterprise" was laid down and the hope was held out for the achievement of justice through the automatic balances of a market economy.

There were both libertarians and equalitarians in the radical forces of the seventeenth-century England and eighteenth-century France. In Cromwell's army the Levellers tended to be libertarians and the "Diggers" equalitarians, and the ideological difference between the preference for liberty and the preference for equality between the middle classes and the poorer classes has been apparent from the Cromwellian to this day. Neither the libertarians nor the equalitarians realized that equality and liberty are in paradoxical relation to each other and that it is possible to purchase the one only at the price of the other. This paradox was obscured by the hope of the libertarians that political liberty would ultimately bring the fruit of equality and by the hope of the equalitarians that the abolition of property would ultimately result in the "withering away of the state."

The libertarians proved more right in the long run than the equalitarians. They had illusions about the immediate efficacy of liberty in creating equal justice, but these illusions were harmless so long as a free society made it possible to create balances of power in both the political and economic sphere which would make for justice. The equalitarians proved themselves wholly wrong because their theories made it possible for a group of elite to establish a monopoly of power in the name of utopia. But the superiority of libertarian over equalitarian liberalism is not as interesting in this context as the fact that both forms of liberalism were abstract and unrealistic in coming to terms with the perennial factors of social hierarchy and social unity and stability, which made liberty and equality the regulative principles but not the realizable goals of the community.

It is rather significant that both the Christian radicals of seventeenth-century England and the secularist radicals of eighteenth-century France were utopian. Perhaps it was not possible to challenge the organic unities and social hierarchies of traditional society without a measure of illusion. Illusion may have been the necessary motive force of social protest. Subsequent history tended to develop a viable form of liberalism which was conscious of both the dangers of an organic unity and an excessive social hierarchy, and of the perennial character of these two phenomena in any community. It also developed a viable conservatism, which was distinguished from a viable liberalism only by an ideologically conditioned emphasis on either the necessity, or the corruption, of these two phenomena.

But in order to analyze these forms of liberalism and conservatism more exactly we must consider the history of liberal and conservative thought in the three great nations—France, Britain, and America—which have given us the most characteristic embodiments of a democratic society. In the American imagination France was the first nation to shatter the mold of an organic aristocratic civilization. It was in fact, however, the second and not the first, the Cromwellian Revolution in England having preceded the French Revolution by more than a century. But meanwhile the Restoration had again put a king on the throne in England. Since monarchy was the symbol of malignant power for both French and American equalitarians and libertarians, the Cromwellian Revolution was forgotten and France became the symbol of the new day of liberty and fraternity both in her own esteem and in ours. This was a pity, for as a matter of fact France also became the embodiment of all abstract liberalism. The first danger of such abstract idealism is that the ideals are not in sufficient contact with reality to engage the stuff of history, and abstract liberalism becomes irrelevant liberalism. The second danger is that an heroic effort will be made to apply the ideal to the social stuff without any recognition of its paradoxical character. French liberalism became involved in both errors.

The first danger came from the attempt to apply the ideals rigorously. Though the revolutionary ferment of the Enlightenment favored libertarianism more than equalitarianism, the actual course of the revolution led to the annulment of liberty and the effort to establish equality by methods which Edmund Burke described as "leveling everything which had raised up its head." The annulment of liberty in the Jacobin fanaticism was the fruit of a simple rationalism, which agreed with the Catholic position that "error" does not have the same right as "truth" and could not imagine any truth contradicting the truth it had perceived. Thus the foundations were laid for what Talmon calls "Totalitarian Democracy." The presuppositions of this kind of democracy naturally led to Bonapartist absolutism. There was no recognition in it of the fragmentary character of all human knowledge and virtue, nor of the necessity of guarding against all centers of power, even if, and particularly when, power pretends to speak in the name of the "people." The communists' version of "people's democracy" reveals that they are quite conscious of the deep affinity and historical connection between the first and the second version of totalitarian democracy.

Idealistic fanaticism, which does not recognize the uses to which ideals may be put, is dangerous. But it is equally dangerous to cover the perennial realities of man's social life with an idealistic slogan. Thus France never "restored" the traditional order as in Britain. But in another sense the revolution had never abolished it. Parliament was governed by revolutionary slogans but the bureaucracy which really governed France frantically preserved the ancient distinctions and inequalities. The rising middle class thought it sufficient to liquidate the aristocracy in order to achieve "equality," but it proved itself desperately anxious to maintain its privileged position against the rising industrial classes. Despite the fact that the freedom of economic enterprise had its inception in the French physiocratic theory, the French business classes were singularly lacking in "enterprise," so that a moribund capitalism, together with the frantic class consciousness of the middle classes, succeeded in driving the industrial workers to revolutionary desperation in a nation which had presumably established liberty and equality. The imperial relations of a technical to a non-technical nation, more specifically the relation of France to North Africa, were also approached in terms of an abstract universalism. Algeria was simply incorporated into Metropolitan France, and this was supposed to satisfy Algerian aspirations. Tragic events of recent history prove that the organic and historic forms of human togetherness cannot be so easily dissolved by abstract individualism and universalism. France as a nation must finally come to terms with the budding nation of Algeria and with the fact that the Algerians cannot be made into Frenchmen by an act of parliament.

Whether it be fair to make France the symbol of an abstract liberalism, it has certainly proved that such liberalism is dangerous whether it believes in the possibility of realizing simply the principles of liberty or equality, or whether it does not really believe in either but merely obscures the actual realities without being critical of them.

England has obviously had some historic advantages over France in coming to terms with the moral realities of an open society. It is not quite clear whether these advantages alone will account for the superior wisdom of English culture in welding the virtues of a traditional civilization with those of a technical one. Some of the advantages derive from the character of the forces operative in the Cromwellian Revolution. They contained not only utopian equalitarians (such as Winstanley) and utopian libertarians such as the Levellers, but independents who genuinely believed in liberty as such and not merely in liberty for themselves. Some of them understood too that liberty can be sustained only by a spirit of tolerance which understands the fragmentary character of all human knowledge, and confesses with John Saltmarsh that "my truth is as dark to thee as thy truth is dark to me until the Lord enlighten all our seeing."

Some of the superior wisdom undoubtedly derives from the remnants of traditional virtues which were represented in the forces of Cromwell's army. There was, for instance, Ireton's shrewd observation that he preferred "the rights of Englishmen to the rights of man," meaning that a mutually acknowledged right and responsibility was a more reliable guarantee of justice than abstractly conceived "inalienable rights." All the superiority of a common law tradition, of an unwritten constitution, and a history in which "liberty broadens down from precedent to precedent" is expressed in this preference.

Some of the superior wisdom may have derived from a man like Richard Hooker, who combined the sense of historical realities with the Thomistic concepts of "natural law," and who thus became the father of both the theories of John Locke, the philosopher of the English Revolution, and of Edmund Burke, the critic of the French Revolution. At any rate, there was enough virtue in the thought and the achievements of a traditional society to permit a "restoration" when the revolutionary fever had spent itself and Cromwell could not maintain himself without annulling democracy. The restoration did not, however, restore the traditional society without embodying the truths and justices of the revolution. It finally led to the constitution of 1688 which not only established William and Mary on the throne, but also added the idea of the people's sovereignty to the idea of monarchy as a symbol of the continuing will of a people as distinct from the momentary will, by which governments were made and unmade. A more pluralistic society was established in this way than by the way of pure revolution, and guards were set up against monopolies of power. Above all, the traditional and inevitable social hierarchies and communal stabilities were protected against too simple applications of the criteria of liberty and equality, while the hierarchies were subjected to the judgement of these criteria of justice and placed under the check of universal suffrage. Thus a community was created which could absorb, and profit from, both the middle-class and the workers' rebellion without rendering the wholeness of a traditional culture and community. This community was in time to confront the world with the spectacle of an aristocratic society quickened, after a terrible war, by the socialist slogan of "fair shares for all." In obedience to that slogan it could set up a welfare state under the aegis of a constitutional monarchy. It could even liquidate an empire and transmute it into a commonwealth of nations. Both a nation and an empire were remolded gradually and therefore more wisely than by revolutionary fanaticism. The organic aspects of community were protected, but their excesses were corrected by the new balances of power made possible in a commercial civilization.

American thought and practice can be understood only as the unique experience of a democracy created on virgin soil and without an aristocratic historical background. But it is also helpful to realize that we have drawn our theories mostly from France and our practice from Britain. The effort to build a balance of power into the very heart of government by the "separation of powers" was a novel invention, drawn from Calvinistic sources. On the whole the founding fathers had a less roseate view of the perfectibility of man than the French philosophers. They therefore wisely took precautions against any monopoly of power establishing itself, including monopolies which tried to speak in the name of the people.

America developed a plutocracy rather than an aristocracy. Although such a society of money power does not have the security of an hereditary aristocracy, we nevertheless had a common-sense appreciation of the requirements of national unity and gradation of authority which went beyond the wisdom of traditional liberalism. Yet we were able to build a remarkably "open" society, partly by grace of an advancing frontier and a continually expanding economy. These favorable circumstances, rather than French prestige, are probably responsible for the note of sentimentality in our political thought. We have regarded both liberty and equality as more easily realizable than they are. But we have realized them beyond the dreams of any European nation. We failed catastrophically only on one point—in our relation to the Negro race. This "American dilemma" is on the way of being resolved, and one of the instruments of its resolution has proved to be the constitutional insistence on equality as a criterion of justice, an insistence which the Supreme Court has recently implemented after generations of hesitation in regard to the application of the principle to our relation with a minority group, which has the advantage of diverging obviously from the dominant type in our nation and which still bears the onus of former subjugation in slavery. At last the seeming sentimentality of the preamble of our Declaration of Independence—the declaration that "all men are created equal"—has assumed political reality and relevance. It is not true that all men are created equal, but the statement is a symbol of the fact that all men are to be treated equally, within the terms of the gradations of function which every healthy society uses for its organization. We have, in other words, done tolerably well in transmuting sentimentalities into relevant criteria of justice. Hence our political thought always lags behind our practice. Our performance is wiser than our theory; and we are more virtuous than we claim to be. We still present ourselves to the world in terms of pure libertarian slogans. Either the world misunderstands us because of these slogans, or it knows us well enough to realize that our achievement has been, not so much the attainment of pure liberty as the attainment of equal justice and social stability within the framework of a free society. But such an appreciation must be gained against the influence of caricatures of ourselves which both we and our communist detractors insist on making.

Both a purely libertarian appreciation and a purely equalitarian criticism of our political realities distort the true picture of American democracy.

JUSTICE TO THE AMERICAN NEGRO FROM STATE, COMMUNITY AND CHURCH

The Supreme Court decision on segregation was not only a milestone in the history of relations between races in our country, but also in the wholesome interaction between the abstract concept of human rights and the specific rights of the American citizen. In spite of the Bill of Rights it required a Civil War to free the Negro from slavery. Soon thereafter it became apparent that the social and moral resources of the nation were insufficient to guarantee him equal standing with other citizens. In a culture that prided itself on its openness and social mobility, the Negro alone was reduced to the status of the medieval serf. In a nation that prided itself on being a melting pot for all the races of men, or rather of Europe, the Negro was prevented by law or by custom from participating in the process. His rights could not be recognized, or made real, until sufficient moral and political vitality in the nation and community insisted that they be.

The Negro was gradually emancipated from his cultural backwardness, partly by the exertions of gifted members of the race who were able to transcend the handicaps of unequal educational opportunities, and partly by the slow development of greater educational opportunities on either a segregated or unsegregated basis. The achievements of the Negro in the arts and in sports have been particularly vivid reminders of the potentialities of a common humanity and a refutation of those who insist on educational inequality as the natural consequence of an inherent inequality.

The cultural factors were not strong enough, however, to close the gap. Before the turn of the century the Supreme Court found it expedient to invent the neat device of "separate but equal" facilities in education, in order to comply with the provisions of the Bill of Rights. The Court thereby proved that it was not sure of the power of the majesty of the law if the law was too far in advance of the historic factors in the community. The device served the nation for half a century, not only to conceal the hiatus between human rights and the rights of Americans, but also to compel the creation of more equal educational opportunities, and indeed of unsegregated education where the community was unable to provide equal facilities.

The turning of the screw of the law tighter and tighter has been so effective in recent decades that many genuine supporters of racial equality regretted that the nation was not allowed to explore this avenue of interaction between law and custom for a few more decades before the Court decreed that separate educational facilities could never be equal since they created the odium of inequality, a psychological factor that no amount of equal equipment could overcome.

The Hard Core of Prejudice

The Court, when challenged by Negroes on the point that

segregated schools could not provide equality in fact, gave the only possible decision and declared that segregated schools did indeed violate the Bill of Rights. One wonders whether this new decision represents a growth in the mind of the Court due to the contemporary climate of opinion, or whether the Court thought that the neat device had served its purpose and, if continued, would do more harm than good.

If one compares the two Court decisions one has a lively sense of the vital relation between juridical decisions and the historic factors that affect those decisions. In that sense the Supreme Court follows the election returns. But while the decision was inevitable, subsequent developments have proved that there is even now no clear supremacy of a law based upon human rights over the mores of a community that does not acknowledge the common humanity of fellow citizens. It is clear that in those portions of the Southern and border states where there was a disposition to establish genuine community across the barriers of racial prejudice, the Court decision gave an added impetus to the process. On the other hand, those counties which had made least progress in integration were prompted to overt defiance by the Court ruling. When this hiatus between the law, embodying an ideal, and the mores of the community is wide, the application of the law case-hardens the hard core of defiance.

This hard core can be defined in almost arithmetical terms. It consists of counties and states in which the Negroes form a very large minority or a majority. In such counties and states the pattern of nullification has already been established. We may be grateful that the pattern is not as widespread as that of the nullification of the franchise after the Fourteenth Amendment. But the fact that it is there, proves the impotence of the concept of human rights if the community does not have the moral and cultural resources to comprehend it. It is to be hoped that the areas of recalcitrance will be geographically so small that the mood of the general community will gradually permeate them and soften their defiance.

The fact that the most explicit defiance occurs also in counties where the cultural and educational standards are lowest gives us some clue to the sources on which race prejudice feeds. Prejudice may of course be any opinion with which we do not agree. Race prejudice may best be defined, however, as primarily group pride, which is almost always an extension of the survival impulse of the group. In the case of Negro-white relations the compound of survival impulse and pride manifests itself in extravagant fears of intermarriage, which is supposed to threaten the white race in its purity. It is worth observing, in countering these fears, that there was a greater mixture of blood in slavery times than in any subsequent period.

The other source of prejudice is the fear of the Negro's cultural backwardness. If we are right in defining this backwardness as cultural rather than biological, it will of course be cured in time by precisely those equal opportunities of education which the Constitution and the Court seek to impose upon the community. But this fact does not immediately help anxious mothers and fathers in those counties of the South which regard a common education as a threat to the cultural adequacy of their children's education.

Great social evils are corrected and social changes made, on the whole, by implicit rather than explicit processes. The law sometimes plays a creative role, as it has in this instance. But usually the law merely regularizes and symbolizes social realities and power relations that have been achieved by gradual accommodation, unless such flagrant injustices have developed in a community that a violent eruption of dissident forces has led to radical change.

The Paradox of the Churches

If we must rely chiefly on the slow erosion of racial prejudice, every common activity of trade or culture in which community is established and men are prompted to recognize a common worth or an uncommon excellence is an important factor. This fact probably explains why the Christian churches in the South have been relatively so impotent in establishing racial brotherhood, despite their explicit universalistic principles. For the churches, as Negro Christians long ago ruefully admitted, have been the most segregated communities in the South and for that matter, in the nation. Nothing can hide the fact that this religiously sanctified racial parochialism has been a grievous offense against the very ideals of the Christian faith. But it has also been the negative by-product of one of the genuine achievements of the sectarian church in our nation: the creation of integral communities on the level of local congregations. Thus we have the ironic fact that the sports fields, theaters, and music halls of the nation have been more creative than the churches in establishing community between the races.

This actual "chumminess" of the local congregation has invalidated the universal principle at the heart of the gospel. Particular brotherhood, ethnically based, has invalidated the universal brotherhood implicit in the Christian ethic.

Not only sports and the theater but also the trade unions have exceeded the achievements of the churches in the field of racial amity. The theater has offered scope for the display of the particular artistic gifts of the Negro race. Many trade unions, particularly in recent decades, have been able to transcend race distinctions in the recognition of common economic needs of the workers. Significantly, the industrial unions which organized the semiskilled workers were more creative than the old craft unions of the AFL, jealous of securities they associated with ethnic privileges. In every case, the contingencies of history in the craft or art were more potent in breaking down the walls of partition than the moral admonitions of the churches or the decrees of the law.

This generalization is subject to qualification in view of the exceptional achievement of the Catholic Church in breaking down the walls of partition. Catholicism has been much more rigorous and successful than the Protestant churches on the racial issue. Partly this success is due to the hierarchial structure of the Church, and the consequent ability of bishops and priests to set standards even in defiance of lay opinion. Catholic schools have been desegregated even when the bishop found it necessary to threaten recalcitrant parents with excommunication.

Democracy and Justice

If one compares the record of this "undemocratic" church with the "democratic" Protestant churches that have the most dismal history of sanctified racial prejudice, one must come to the conclusion that absolute democracy is not necessarily a resource of justice. It sacrifices leadership to lay prejudice, and obscures the continuing and broadly based will of the national community to assert the immediate and particular will of the local community. Many clergymen in the Protestant churches have been as right and as heroic as the Catholic priests. But the bishops have supported the priests while Protestant congregations have been free to dismiss their clergy when they were critical of the "Southern way of life."

The Catholic Church brings to issue the inclusive community of a sacramental rather than a chummy fellowship. The fellowship of the Protestant Church is always degenerating into a sanctified sense of kind, whether of race or class or neighborhood. The sacramental dimensions of the Catholic communion enlarge the communion of saints and conform it more nearly to the universal dimension intended in the gospel.

If one analyzes the contributions of Catholicism to racial amity, one must be struck by the similarity between its contribution and that of the Bill of Rights. In both cases, one secular and the other religious, one political and the other ecclesiastical, the norm is imposed from above upon a recalcitrant democracy. Perhaps this is just another proof that we must approach this vexing problem from above and from below, both by the authoritative affirmation of norms and by the gradual achievement of community through common interests and pressures.

The Catholic approach is from above if we measure the immediate resources of the people in a community, their fears and ambitions, their hatreds and their loves. It is from below if we count the religious institution as one of the cultural forces within the community that make it possible for the community to achieve the ideal which the Constitution has embodied into the basic law. Our Bill of Rights placed us in the same dilemma as the Children of Israel. We were committed to an ideal in principle that we were almost bound to contradict in practice. Fortunately, we did not absolutely contradict it. If there had been no moral vitality in our culture we would have continued in the evasion of the law initiated after the Civil War, when the vanquished were forced to give the slaves their freedom but could not long be forced to let them retain the vote which alone could provide political substance to that freedom. But the vitality of the national culture is finding ways of evading the evasion.

7

THE RELATIONS OF CHRISTIANS AND
JEWS IN WESTERN CIVILIZATION

The long and tragic history of the relations of the Christian majority to the Jewish minority in Western Christian civilization should prompt more humility and self-examination among Christians than is their wont. Whether we judge these relations in terms of the terrible excesses of the counter-reformation in Spain or the Nazi terror; or in terms of the normal intolerance of an authoritarian Catholicism of Medieval Europe with its Jewish ghettos; or in terms of the frustrated zeal of Protestant pietism, which cannot understand the stubbornness of the Jew in resisting conversion; or in terms of the residual anti-semitism of the most liberal societies, we have conclusive evidence that the Christian faith has not had enough grace to extend genuine community to the Jew, despite the fact (or possibly because of the fact) that the two religions have a common bible and a common historical approach to the ultimate.

The Jews are probably in error in attributing the sad state of affairs to specifically Christian deficiencies; for this history simply proves the perpetual pride of any majority dealing with any minority. But the Christians are certainly too complacent about the failure of their allegedly superior universal faith to inculcate a charity which transcends the religious community. The well-known universalism of Paul, "In Christ there is neither Jew nor Greek, neither bond nor free," does not help in the problem of the relation of two religious communities to each other.

There has been considerable debate among both Christians and Jews whether anti-semitism is prompted chiefly by religious or by ethnic prejudices. These debates have been on the whole uninteresting because it is so obvious that the prejudice against the Jew arises from the fact that he is *both* ethnically and religiously peculiar and stubbornly resists assimilation, *both* ethnically and religiously.

It is this two-fold divergence from dominant type which is the Jews' chief offence in the eyes of the majority. Jews ought to admit that we are dealing with a human problem rather than a peculiarly Christian problem. For they could not have preserved their integrity as a people throughout the centuries without enforcing their endogamous rules through the sense of their own superiority. In cases of intermarriage the opposition from Jewish parents has usually been as persistent as, if not even more stubborn than, that of the Christian parents. We are dealing with the problem of the moral capacity of collective man; and we find that the survival impulse in both minority and majority is bound to make use of all spiritual factors available to it. We cannot live and survive collectively without using group prides as instruments of survival. In the case of our own nation, which prides itself on being a melting pot assimilating all ethnic groups, there is no question of the survival impulse of the Aryan majority. It refuses to assimilate the Negro because it has the sense of the survival of a pure white majority and fears intermarriage with an ethnic group which diverges so obviously from type. But in the case of the Jew it resents his refusal to be assimilated and fails to understand the peculiar problems of a peculiar people who have miraculously survived for two thousand years without a homeland, living under the hazards of the diaspora in many nations and cultures.

The problem of the Christian majority, particularly in America, is therefore to come to terms with the stubborn will to live of the Jews as a peculiar people, both religiously and ethnically. The problem can be solved only if the Christian and Gentile majority accepts this fact and ceases to practice tolerance provisionally in the hope that it will encourage assimilation ethnically and conversion religiously.

Such provisional tolerance always produces violent reactions when ultimately disappointed, as in the case of Luther, who thought that the Jews had refused to become Catholic but would undoubtedly accept the purer Protestant version of the Christian faith. The Christian majority can achieve a more genuine tolerance only if it assumes the continued refusal of the Jew to be assimilated, either ethnically or religiously. That recognition involves an appreciation of the resources of Jewish life, morally and religiously, which make Judaism something other than an inferior form of religion such as must ultimately recognize the superiority of the Christian faith; and end its long resistance by capitulation and conversion.

We must consider the task of achieving this kind of toleration in both the moral and the religious spheres. In the moral sphere the Christian majority is bound to re-examine its presuppositions, which either encourage or fail to discourage the widespread conviction that Jews tend to be sharp to the point of dishonesty in business; and which fail to note that the Jews have in fact a superior capacity for civic virtue which the Gentile majority rather flagrantly overlooks.

In regard to the charge of dishonesty, a part of the difficulty no doubt derives from the old hazard of collective relations. That hazard is that a dubious action in our own group is not regarded as typical but unique while the same action by an individual of another group is regarded as typical. Thus, when a very prominent Christian banker was sent to Sing Sing on a serious charge several years ago, no one declared that his defalcation was typical of Christian bankers. A similar offence by a Jewish banker would have invariably become the base for a false syllogism.

But more specific historical sources have contributed to this prejudice about the character of Jewish business life. The sources have their origin in Medieval Europe. The Jews were excluded from the professions and the ownership of land. Therefore, only trade was open to them as a means of livelihood. Moreover, they were forced into the profession of banking by a curious irony of legalism. For the prohibition of usury, originally derived from the Old Testament, was enforced upon Christians; but it did not bind the Jews because the prohibition was confined to the Jewish community. The Jews consequently became the money-lenders of the medieval economy and earned the disrespect both of the landed aristocrat and of the lower non-commercial classes. Salo Baron points out the Jewish business men in the Middle Ages frequently achieved a high social status, just below the aristocracy. But the social status could not prevent the prejudice against them, particularly since their success in banking and commerce seemed to validate the charge of dishonesty to non-commercial classes. For since Aristotle, both classical antiquity and medieval Christianity had a prejudice against the "huckster."

The medieval prejudice had a very stubborn life. It was transferred to America by the populist movement, which found the very non-medieval farmer just as prejudiced against the money-lender and trader as the medieval peasant. Thus a very powerful stereotype was generated which outlasted medieval culture and has served as the instrument of the sense of moral superiority of the majority group even in liberal cultures in which Jews gradually acquired political rights. In non-liberal or traditional cultures such as those of Poland and Russia this prejudice was maintained despite the fact that the Ghettos developed an impressively unworldly and unprudential spirituality, in comparison with which Gentile behavior would seem flagrantly worldly and prudential.

As illustrating the power of stereotypes, may I be autobiographical and report an experience of my youth? In the Middle-Western town where I spent my childhood there were two prominent Jews. One was a clothing merchant, respected by everyone and deserving of respect. He was public-spirited, honest and generous, and his approach to his fellow men had something of the old-world courtliness in it. Everybody said how nice he was and wasn't it remarkable that he was not at all typically Jewish? Not knowing many Jews we did not know in what sense he was atypical or unique. He simply did not conform to the stereotype. The other Jew was a very successful business man who began life as a peddler. He had phenomenal success, and that success was assumed to prove his dishonesty, even though there was no evidence of dishonesty anywhere in his record. But he was inclined to display his wealth and to obscure as much as possible his lowly origin. All these human frailties made him in the mind of our community a "typical" Jew rather than a unique one.

But the unfavorable judgement upon the business ethics of the Jews, made by most Gentiles, is not as prejudiced as the inability of the Christian community to give the Jew credit for his undoubted capacity for civic virtue which equals, and frequently exceeds, that of the Christian community. My first personal acquaintance with this capacity was occasioned by my experience as a young pastor in Detroit, where I served as the chairman of the Mayor's commission on race and had as my vice-chairman a Jewish lawyer, who combined a sophisticated knowledge of human nature with a broad charity. He was realistic almost to the point of cynicism, yet his realism did not tempt to cynicism. Rather it generated both charity and the spirit of justice in him. If one claims that the Jewish capacity for civic virtue frequently excels that of Christians, the claim rests upon the Jewish capacity for critical devotion to the community which frequently excels the more traditional loyalties of the Gentile community and the typical benevolent goodness of the Christian business man. My judgements may be colored by years of political activity, left of center. Whether the problem was one of challenging a nationalist isolationism or of amending the traditional libertarian attitudes of the business community, Jewish men of wealth were more emancipated from the prejudice of their class than Christian business men. They were more discriminate in their judgements of social policy. They were usually also more generous in the support of communal projects which transcended the loyalties of a particular group.

Two possible causes for this capacity for civic virtue might be given. The one reaches deeply into the past and the other is very contemporary. The cause deriving from the past may well be what has been defined as the "Prophetic" passion for justice. The prophets of Israel did not define justice as neatly as Aristotle did. But they defined it more relevantly. For according to the prophets of Israel the justice of God was critical of the elders, the judges and the princes because they "turned aside the needy at the gates," because "the spoil of the poor was in their houses"; because they "sold the needy for a pair of shoes"; in short, the prophetic analysis of the problems of the community was the beginning of the realism which knew that power was never completely in the service of justice. Therefore, the powerful would be judged more severely than the poor. Justice was not equal justice but a bias in favor of the poor. Justice always leaned toward mercy for the widows and the orphans. The prophetic sense of justice was in short relevant to the perennial problems of the human community where power is needed to establish order but always exacts too high a price in justice for its services.

If the prophetic sense of justice was more existential than the speculations of Greek philosophers, it may also be true that it was more relevant to the problems of the community than the Christian ideal of love. This may be true despite the fact that the prophets drew no sharp distinction between love and justice and that the double love commandment of Jesus was drawn from Old Testament sources. But the Christian idea of love, being drawn from the example of Jesus' sacrifice is usually interpreted in terms of such selflessness that it has application purely to individual and not to collective situations. In collective situations justice is achieved by an equilibrium of power, by a balance of social forces; and Christian idealism

has had difficulty in incorporating the discriminations necessary for the achievement of such equilibria into its systems of
thought. Both Protestant liberalism with its undue optimism
about the moral capacities of men, and Lutheran conservatism, with its undue pessimism about collective possibilities
of justice, have failed to solve this problem. Ironically enough,
the most profound elaboration of the biblical love doctrine
has been made by a contemporary Jewish philosopher, Martin
Buber; but he unfortunately exhibits the same difficulties in
coming to terms with the ethics of all collective and institutional relations as Protestant doctrine. Thus, Emil Brunner
drew upon the thought of Buber in order to establish a typically Lutheran distinction between love and justice, which
made love into the moral norm for purely personal and
intimate relations. But in this sphere Buber is not typically
Jewish. The social ethic of Christianity has always been
troubled by the fact that it is difficult to derive a social ethic
from the *Agape* concept of the gospels. A social ethic demands
not unprudential heedlessness but discriminate judgements.
From Bernard of Clairvaux to the modern Christian philanthropist it has been difficult for Christian thought to avoid
the danger of making almsgiving or philanthropy into a
substitute for discriminate justice. Perhaps it is necessary
to add that a religious ethic, whether Jewish or Christian,
has some difficulties with the discriminations which justice
requires. This is why a certain amount of secularism was
necessary before these problems of justice in a complex technical society could be solved. The more discrimination becomes necessary in the adjudication of rights and interests
the less can the original religio-ethical impulse be counted on
to establish a brotherly justice. For justice is at once the

servant of love and an approximation to love under institutional conditions. The superiority of the Jew's sense of justice may be derived from the fact that his norms were elaborated in a communal situation while the Christian norms transcend all communities. Ideally a new community, the church, was built to incarnate them. But the community beyond the church has remained an enigma to the Christian conscience.

It would be unfair however to attribute the superiority, if any, of the Jew to these ancient sources when more contemporary sources are more obvious. The Jewish superiority in civic virtue, if any, rests, according to the testimony of many objective observers, primarily upon their status as a minority group. They have the same superiority as other minority groups, including women. They may be loyal Americans or citizens of other nations, but they stand slightly on the outside, as a minority, and the critical detachment of their status gives them a resource which saves them from their traditionalism in accepting the standards of their community. That is why they stand slightly left of center in any political spectrum.

That is also why the Jews have been so helpful to the Negroes in achieving the status of equal citizenship in a national community in which the Jew was regarded with suspicion for being too smart and the Negro with condescension as being not smart enough for the American amalgam. The benefactions of the Jewish philanthropist, Julius Rosenwald, in favor of Negro education may be regarded as symbols of this peculiar affinity between two minorities in the national community. The more competent minority felt a kinship with the less competent minority.

In explaining the "liberal" tendencies of Jewish business

men in the days of the "New Deal" a Jewish business man explained, "We Jews have a more insistent interest in the health of our society because we know that if the society becomes sick it may become hysterical; and as a minority we do not feel safe in any hysterical society." The sickness in Germany gave point to this observation about the Jew's stake in the health of any community.

An analysis of the prejudices and misconceptions as between the two religions in the moral and political sphere may be in accord with the principle of applying the ultimate test: "By their fruits shall ye know them." But it can only be preliminary to a consideration of the relation of the two biblical faiths, with a view to achieving more charity and understanding between them. The misunderstandings are a scandal not only because the two faiths have a common bible, but because they share the spiritual guidance of Western democracy, more particularly in our own nation. Professor Toynbee has devoted his Gifford Lectures to the problem of religious toleration. But in that book he illustrates the complexity of our problem. For his primary purpose is to achieve more understanding between Christianity and Mahayana Buddhism. Yet he consistently misinterprets the Jewish faith and culture and exhibits facets of prejudice which make understanding more difficult between two faiths which share a common bible and a common Western civilization. We are not dealing with the problems of world community only, but with our own national community when we strive for a better understanding between Jew and Christian.

It is a commonplace to emphasize the common rigorous monotheism when we seek to enumerate the affinities between the two religions. We would give a more adequate description of the affinities and be introduced to the hazards of the relation between the two religions if we emphasized that the two faiths share not only a common monotheism but a common attitude toward history, toward historic responsibilities and toward our relation to the creator God as a sovereign of history.

This common historical attitude contains one of our deepest perplexities, because both religions accept a particular event in history as the ultimate disclosure of the eternal mystery for us; yet they accept by faith different revelatory events. Both faiths ought probably to admit more readily that their attitude toward historic revelation, which is accepted by faith and cannot be compelled by reason or achieved by mystic experience, contains both the secret of their creativity on the historical scene and the offense both to the Greeks and to modern culture which tries in its various scientific and philosophic pursuits to reduce the mystery of the divine to rational intelligibility; and in the process it inevitably obscures the depth of the divine mystery and makes the world processes self-explanatory and self-fulfilling.

But both faiths derive not only their ethical creativity and their life-affirming impulse from the acceptance in faith of an historical revelation. They also derive the perils of religious caprice and obscurantism from this reliance on historic revelation. How is the claim to be validated, in the one case that Israel is the chosen people of God, and in the other case that "God was in Christ reconciling the world unto himself"? Professor Toynbee heedlessly derives all religious fanaticism from the Jewish adventure of faith, but does not recognize that the second covenant is just as fruitful of fanatic claims as the first. Both covenants assume that an historic fact is more than a mere fact; it is but a disclosure of the mystery which bares history. In both cases a community of believers is organized on the basis of faith's apprehension of the revelatory depth of the fact. In both cases the burden of proof is on the covenant community that this exclusively apprehended revelation does not imply an exclusive God; but that we have actually to do with the mysterious creator of the universe and the sovereign of history. In both cases the only proof of the affirmation of faith must be "witness," the witness of life, which is oriented not to some private and peculiar God, but to the divine sovereign who is equally rigorous in his demands upon believers and upon unbelievers and offers no special security to the elect. Whether or not the believer is subject to this God and responds to him in faithfulness and repentance, in gratitude and hope, can only be proved by the quality of a life. Both covenant faiths must bear witness to their revelation. Both faiths are in danger of neglecting the scientific and metaphysical tests for universal validity, which, incidentally, may eliminate caprice but are always in danger of annulling both the mystery of man, who transcends the coherences of nature and reason; and the mystery of history, which is a realm of both divine and human freedom.

Thus we see that provisionally both faiths exhibit the same resources and are exposed to the same hazards. They are very similar but also very different. Can we deal with these differences in terms which will enhance understanding and not create misunderstanding? Let us begin, both Christian and Jew, by admitting that the commitment of faith does not permit a completely objective view. The presuppositions on the basis of which we reason, determine the reasoning not only of those who are explicitly religious but of all secular faiths. We who are committed to an historic faith are usually regarded as arbitrary by scientists and philosophers. But these, though having no explicit faith, have their own implicit presuppositions. We cannot climb over our presuppositions but we need not be their prisoners. If we were absolutely prisoners there would be no solution for the problem of fanaticism.

Judaism and Christianity are two covenant faiths, in which a community of believers propagates the shared faith and seeks to bear witness to its validity even to those who do not share it. But the covenants and the faiths are different. Let us try as objectively as possible to analyze these differences. The differences may conveniently be studied in three categories: 1) the problem of Messianism, 2) the problem of grace and law, and 3) the problem of particularity and universality.

1. The most obvious difference between the two faiths was stated succinctly by Martin Buber. He declared: "To the Christian, the Jew is the stubborn fellow who is still waiting for the Messiah; to the Jew, the Christian is the heedless fellow who in an unredeemed world declares that redemption has somehow or other taken place." This difference would remain, even if we eliminated from the Christian record those passages in the Johannine gospel in which the opposition is stylized and stereotyped in the phrase "The Jews," a phrase which undoubtedly obscures the fact that in the founding of the new covenant community there were Jews in both the opposition and the new community of believers. Incidentally those Jews are probably in error who would eliminate prejudice by emphasizing that it was the Romans who killed Jesus. For that emphasis would not obscure the fact that we are dealing with a religious drama in the Jewish community.

Nothing of this kind will obscure the fact that the Christian community accepted a crucified prophet, who may or may not have been informed by a Messianic consciousness and regarded the whole drama of his life, death and resurrection (about which as a public historic event there is incidentally some question) as the fulfillment of Messianic prophecy. We need not take too seriously the charge of Toynbee that the Jews in rejecting Jesus turned their back on the insights of their own prophetic heritage. Jesus was obviously not the Messiah whom the Jews expected. Even if the Messianic claims of the church had not been elaborated in terms of Greek metaphysics and finally defined in the Nicene Creed, the idea of Jesus as the final revelation of the divine would have been unacceptable to normative Judaism. It would have seemed to violate their rigorous monotheism even without the explicit trinitarian formula of the creeds. The offence lay primarily in the crucified rather than in the triumphant Messiah; and in the assertion that in the drama of his crucifixion, we have a revelation of the divine mercy in which God takes the sins of the world upon himself. This affirmation is freely confessed by Paul as being "to the Jews a stumbling-block." It does not follow with logical necessity from anything predicted in Messianic hopes, though the Christian community (rightly I believe) saw it as a fulfillment of the quasi-Messianic conception in the Second Isaiah of the "suffering servant." If it was actually Israel which Deutero-Isaiah envisaged in the concept, the appropriation by the church will be the more offensive to the Jew, while being plausible to Christians on the ground that no people but only a single individual could possibly correspond to the conception of the suffering servant.

But the heart of the Messianic issue between Judaism and Christianity is in the observation of Buber. "To the Jew, the Christian is the heedless fellow, who in an unredeemed world affirms that redemption has somehow or other taken place." This indeed is the truth because the Christological center of the Christian faith lies in the assertion that God has been finally and definitely revealed in the Christ drama, and that the burden of that revelation is the divine mercy and forgiveness, which completes what human striving can never complete, since all human efforts and all historic achievements remain ambiguous to the end of history. The idea of the second coming of the Son of Man at the end of history in the New Testament places the two faiths in somewhat similar positions with regard to the character of the historical process, though the emphasis on the Anti-Christ at the end of history in the New Testament reinforces the idea that history will never solve the problem of history, since the contradictions will be heightened rather than diminished. The real difference in Messianism in the two faiths is the idea in the New Testament that the meaning of life in history and the relation of history to its divine ground have been fully revealed in Christ, though the meaning will not be fulfilled till the end of history. From the Christian standpoint this means a radical rejection of utopianism, and with it the hope of the Kingdom of God on earth. From the Jewish standpoint it may mean a relaxation of the ethical tension in history. Buber in his *Paths to Utopia* shows that utopianism is in principle more at home in Jewish than in Christian thought, though the sectarian utopians of Cromwellian England show that there must always be in Christian thought a place for the prayer "Thy kingdom come, thy will be done on earth as it is in heaven."

On the other hand, even the earliest forms of Hebraic Messianism, that of the First Isaiah for instance, had guards against utopianism because they did not expect the Kingdom of God except in a transfigured nature-history. The difference is one of emphasis and there is no radical contrast. The difference in the answer to the problem of history corresponds to the difference in the diagnosis of the human situation. Some Jews have made much of the Christian pessimism implied in the doctrine of "original sin" and have contrasted Jewish optimism with this pessimism. But the weight of evidence is that there is not very much difference between the doctrine of the *Yecer hara* and that of original sin. Jesus incidentally held the Jewish doctrine of the *yecer* and only Paul propounded the doctrine of original sin, relying on the story of the fall, which, after being recorded in Genesis had remarkably little currency in Jewish thought until later apocalyptic writings, from which Paul undoubtedly derived it. In short, there are differences in emphasis in both the diagnoses of the human situation and the religious assurances corresponding to the diagnoses. But there is no simple contrast.

2. The second main issue between Christianity and Judaism concerns the nature of law and the relation of grace to law. As to the former, it is usually assumed by Christians that the law, roughly equated with the decalogue, gives the minimal and negative requirements of righteousness to which the New Testament added the positive norm of love, particularly that reckless love which is characteristic of the Sermon on the Mount. This is the burden of the series of sayings: "It has been said to you of old—but I say unto you." Actually the contrast is not as absolute as Christians suppose. For the

love commandment is taken from the Old Testament and the Rabbis have taught consistently that love is the fulfillment of the law. The Jew when dealing with the problem of moral norms may well question whether the absolute requirements of the Sermon, involving non-resistance and sacrificial love, are guides to ordinary conduct. Shirley Jackson Case, representing the desperate effort of liberal Protestantism to relate this reckless ethic to the ordinary prudence of a social ethic, came to the conclusion that it grew out of the simplicities of a pastoral economy and that we would have to adjust it to the complexities of an industrial civilization.

Karl Barth was certainly nearer to the truth when he defined the ethic as "eschatological" and declared that it was directly relevant to no historic or social situation at all. "Eschatological" may be the wrong word for the definition of the ethic. C. H. Dodd in *The Gospel and the Law* observes that the ethical requirements of the sermon are not eschatological because the demand to turn the other cheek and go a second mile are not meant for an ideal situation. They are meant for the world in which we encounter evil men. The requirements, declares Dodd, give us the direction in which ethical conduct must move. They define, in short, the ethics in the nth degree. Windisch in his *Sermon on the Mount* enumerates many of the teachings of the more rigorous Rabbis which fall into the same category. He suggests, in fact, that Matthew had an ideological interest in establishing Jesus as a new law-giver who was more rigorous than any of the Jewish interpreters of the law. This tendency is partly responsible for the absolute prohibition of divorce, in contrast to Moses, who allowed divorce "for the hardness of your hearts." The Christian Church, particularly Catholicism, has involved itself in many absurdities by this rigorous form of legalism. Let us assume that Christianity raises the moral pinnacle more consistently than Judaism. But let us also admit that there is a tendency in both faiths to climb the moral pinnacle to the ultimate degree. And let us further observe that such a rigorous ethic complicates the problem of a social ethic which must incorporate prudence and a rational adjudication of competing rights. The perennial problem of pacifism in Christianity and also in Judaism, and the wider problem of sectarian rigorism and ascetic withdrawal, common to both religions, but more pronounced in Christianity, prove that it is not possible to survey the moral possibilities of the individual to the nth degree without sacrificing some responsibilities for the order and justice of the community. It will come as a shock to many Christians that the demand of Jesus "Be ye therefore perfect, even as your Father in heaven is perfect" has been a source of much moral confusion, of more confusion than the Old Testament demand, "Be ye therefore holy as I am holy." Some of this confusion can be eliminated if Professor Torrey is correct in his surmise that the actual Aramaic words of Jesus, which were rendered by the Greek "perfection," were "Let your love therefore be all-inclusive as God's love includes all." This would make the demand a part of the consistent love-universalism of Jesus. It is still a part of the ethics in the nth degree, but its emphasis is horizontal and historical rather than vertical and other-worldly. It is therefore more relevant to the problem of communal justice than "perfection," which is usually interpreted in terms of inner purity of motive.

In regard to the law we therefore arrive at the provisional

conclusion that the main outline of the law, as embodied in the decalogue, is accepted by Christians as valid; that the idea of love as the fulfillment of the law is more explicitly stated in the New Testament; but that the heightening of the *Agape* norm until it reaches sacrificial and forgiving love is elaborated in the New Testament so that it explores the final ethical possibilities of the individual, but probably to the embarrassment of an adequate social ethic. Here there are differences but no contrasts.

But the real problem arises in regard to the *halakah*, the details of Jewish legalism, including dietary and sabbath laws, which play such a large part in Jewish moral and spiritual life and which concern the Christian not at all. He simply follows the admonition of Paul: "Stand fast therefore in the freedom with which Christ has made you free." The underlying assumption is that the law is used in Judaism as a guarantee of righteousness and that there is no such guarantee, but that man must rely ultimately upon divine forgiveness. There is, in short, no moral solution for the moral problem of life. The Christian feels himself emancipated from the law. He is probably oblivious to the resources of grace which have been exhibited in Jewish legalism; but he is also bound to observe the embarrassment of many morally sensitive Jews, some secularized, but some like Buber genuinely religious, who have difficulty in regarding the *halakah* as morally relevant. One might mention the protest against this legalism by such an impressive Jewish humanist and humanitarian as Victor Gollancz in his *Dear Timothy*. But the problem of the scope of the law is probably but a facet of the larger problem of the relation of grace to law. Christianity distinguishes itself, in its own mind, from Judaism as a religion of grace rather than of law.

The Johannine gospel states the distinction, from the standpoint of the New Testament, rather flatly: "The law was given by Moses but grace and truth came through Jesus Christ." The question is what we Christians mean by "grace." Since the word has been subject to many interpretations, not all of them valid, let us begin by defining grace as having to do, not with moral norms, but with moral dynamics. The problem of grace looms so large in the New Testament because the diagnosis of the human situation includes an analysis of what Augustine has defined as the "defect of the will," a situation of self-contradiction in the self, which Paul describes in the words, "the good that I would I do not do, and the evil that I would not, that I do."

This confession of impotence is probably the most significant characteristic of Pauline Christianity. It is from the diagnosis of impotence that the doctrine of grace achieves its significance; for grace is the answer to the human problem. Grace is consistently both power and pardon. The Reformation insisted that it was above all pardon and that it was power insofar as the assurance of forgiveness healed the anxious soul of man and emancipated him from preoccupation with self, including preoccupation with his own righteousness. The Christian must not claim that redemption is unknown in Judaism, or that there is not a fully elaborated doctrine of the divine mercy in its relation to the divine justice, even if he believes that this relation, explicated in the Old Testament, is fully defined in the New Testament doctrine of the atonement. I speak as a Christian, of course, when I affirm that on this issue many Christians see the most striking difference between Christianity as a religion of redemption and Judaism as a religion of law.

From the standpoint of the Christian, the doctrine of grace

is the most significant distinction between Christianity and Judaism. But before we claim superiority as Christians because we regard the Christian diagnosis of the human situation as more adequate for us, we must recognize that all Christian conceptions of grace as power, enabling us to do what is right, are no guarantee that we are in possession of such a power. Grace is an accretion of power to the will. Saving grace may be the fruit of the soul's intimate relation with the divine source. There is no doctrine which can guarantee such power. Perhaps it would be well as both Christians and Jews to acknowledge that modern psychiatry and the social sciences have validated the efficacy of "common grace" more explicitly than any saving grace which we may claim as religious people. It is a simple observable fact that we have the capacity to love only as we have the security of the love of others. It is this security which is the real source of grace to most people. It is a grace which can be meditated by any one, religious or irreligious, who is capable of love. Religious faith, of course, tends to lift the security of love above and beyond the vicissitudes of our earthly friendships and thus emancipates us from the failure of our human companions. It is nevertheless true that the most potent form of divine grace is that which is mediated by human love.

It is almost inevitable that we as Christians should claim uniqueness for our faith as a religion of redemption. But we must not claim moral superiority because of this uniqueness. For the efficacy of common grace and the necessity of rational discrimination in all problems of justice do not give a religion of grace that practical superiority over a religion of law which we are inclined to assume. The fact that Jews have been rather more creative than Christians in establishing brotherhood with the Negro, and have done so particularly in a part of the country where the grace of a new life in Christ has been proclaimed in the experience of conversion in the sects of Protestantism, may prove that "saving grace" may be rather too individualistically conceived in Christianity to deal with collective evil. In short, if we measure the two faiths by their moral fruits, the Jewish faith does not fall short, particularly in collective moral achievement, whatever the superior insights of the Christian faith may be in measuring the inner contradictions of the human spirit and in establishing the weakness of his moral will, and the spiritual force to overcome the defect of the will.

3) The third great complex of issues between Christianity and Judaism centers in the problem of particularity and universality. It is probably this problem which prompted Toynbee to suggest that the Jews, in rejecting Jesus, turned their backs on the insights of their great prophets. Obviously the Jewish faith is not universal in the sense of being missionary and offering its way of life to all people. Yet it is universal in the sense that it worships a God who is the sovereign of all nations and offers no special security to Israel. One might argue that the Jews have enlisted the divine so little for their own political survival that they have been homeless for two thousand years. They have, of course, been forced to make their piety into an instrument of collective survival in the diaspora. They could in fact not have survived as a purely secular nation. From the Christian standpoint, the Jews seem to be a nation which has tried desperately to be a church throughout the ages. This is involved in the tension of having a potentially universal religion standing on the historic base of a particular nation. It is this situation which persuaded Franz

Rosenzweig to define the relation of Christianity and Judaism as two religions with one center, worshiping the same God, but with Christianity serving the purpose of carrying the prophetic message to the Gentile world. The definition will not satisfy Christians for it obscures some of the real differences between the two religions; but it is better than almost all alternative definitions of the relation between Jew and Christian, it does do justice to the fact that Christianity is basically Hebraic in genius and that the Hellenic elements in its amalgam have not seriously changed the Hebraic base. It is certainly a better definition than those which prompt Christian missionary activity among the Jews. Our analysis assumes that these activities are wrong not only because they are futile and have little fruit to boast for their exertions. They are wrong because the two faiths despite differences are sufficiently alike for the Jew to find God more easily in terms of his own religious heritage than by subjecting himself to the hazards of guilt feeling involved in a conversion to a faith, which whatever its excellencies, must appear to him as a symbol of an oppressive majority culture. Both Jews and Christians will have to accept the hazards of their historic symbols. These symbols may be the bearers of an unconditioned message to the faithful. But to those outside the faith they are defaced by historic taints. Practically nothing can purify the symbol of Christ as the image of God in the imagination of the Jew from the taint with which ages of Christian oppression in the name of Christ tainted it. This is not merely an historic matter. We are reminded daily of the penchant of anti-semitic and semi-fascist groups, claiming the name of Christ for their campaigns of hatred.

Rosenzweig's definition of the relation may do better than

any other for the two religions, but it does not solve the problem of the Jews insofar as they are both a religious and an ethnic community. Many Christians are pro-Zionist in the sense that they believe that a homeless people require a homeland; but we feel as embarrassed as anti-Zionist religious Jews when Messianic claims are used to substantiate the right of the Jews to the particular homeland in Palestine; or when it is assumed that this can be done without injury to the Arabs.

History is full of strange configurations. Among them is the thrilling emergence of the State of Israel, as a kind of penance of the world for the awful atrocities committed against the Jews; and as a community in which secular and religious forces have been curiously commingled and in such a way that the homeland could not have been established in Palestine except for religious memories and could not be maintained as a workable nation if modern secularism (of which the Prime Minister, Ben-Gurion, is a convenient symbol) had not leavened the lump of Orthodoxy sufficiently to free a modern state from the legal norms which were handed down in tradition from a pastoral community thousands of years ago. These are complications so great that the indifferent outsider will be tempted to laugh at the anachronisms; and the hostile critic will be unduly critical of the Jewish political will to survive. One of Toynbee's most fantastic judgements upon the Jews is his opinion that in "the Last Judgment," the Nazis will be judged more severely, not for having well nigh exterminated the Jews, but for having "tempted the remnant of Jewry to stumble," that is to fight for their lives rather than espouse the "way of gentleness" which presumably means, having failed to adopt a pacifism, which neither Christianity nor Judaism ever consistently espoused. The Jewish nation was formed, partly by the heroic fight for survival of the Jewish people and partly by the sympathies of the Western nations, possibly absolving their conscience for their involvement in the evil of Nazism. It is a glorious moral and political achievement. But a sympathetic Christian cannot but observe that the Jewish ethic and faith, so impressively universal in the diaspora, so fruitful in leavening Western civilization, is not morally safe when it becomes embodied in a nation like all other nations, and when in fighting for the survival of that nation, it comes in conflict with Arab forces. Significantly, Martin Buber's religious Zionism and his effort to establish a bi-national state with the Arabs must come to nothing. Political choices are always more limited than our moral and religious ideas find convenient. The State of Israel is not a religious state; and if it were there would be a danger that it might become a sacerdotal state, because the religious forces in it would be heedless of the hundreds of years of Western history which proved even to the devout that politics, particularly in a technical and complex society, must be secular lest primitive religious loyalties corrupt the character of its justice.

As Christians, we owe the Jew both gratitude for his "prophetic" contribution to our common civilization and understanding of his impulse to build a homeland for a homeless people; and appreciation for the remarkable feat of statesmanship which has provided a home for the homeless. But all this cannot obscure the unsolved problem of particularity and universality of the Jewish people. We ought not to demand that the problem be solved. It is in fact insoluble. For a thousand years the Jews have served our common civilization by exploiting the universalistic implications of their faith. If now after the terrible holocaust of the past decades they, or some of them, should function as a nation and not a church, we Christians can appreciate the impulse and the achievements which are the fruits of the impulse. But the "Council of Judaism" is right when it insists that the two achievements in particularity and universality must not be confused or the prestige of the one be made the servant of the other.

A Christian contemplation of the Jewish problem of particularity and universality will tempt to self-righteousness on the part of the Christian, who is informed by a faith in which the problem is solved in principle, if he does not understand that history is full of realities which violate solutions in principle. The history of Christianity abounds in examples of the use of the Christian faith to exalt or to protect a particular community. The Irish struggle is aggravated by the fact that the Scots-Irish of Northern Ireland are Protestant, while the Southern Irish are Catholic. In the Balkans, the Roman and the Orthodox versions of Christianity are intimately merged with national survival impulses. Even in our nation, priding itself on its melting pot, the Protestant faith is undoubtedly an instrument of pride and cohesion for the North European or "Nordic" groups, as distinguished from the Slavs and the Latins. Every Protestant denomination has some particular ethnic or historical particularity.

We are dealing with a universal, rather than a Jewish, problem. Recognizing that fact will dissipate self-righteousness. But still there is the Jewish problem of particularity and universality. We ought to recognize that among the many illogical emergences of history (that is, configurations which do not fit into our logic) there is the strange miracle of the Jewish people, outliving the hazards of the diaspora for two millennia and finally offering their unique and valuable contributions to the common Western civilization, particularly in the final stage of its liberal society. We should not ask that this peculiar historical miracle fit into any kind of logic or conform to some historical analogy. It has no analogy. It must be appreciated for what it is.

8

THE IMPULSE FOR PERFECTION AND THE
IMPULSE FOR COMMUNITY

The yearning for perfection is undoubtedly deeply embedded in the religious impulse. In the New Testament it is classically expressed in the admonition of Christ: "Be ye therefore perfect, even as your Father in heaven is perfect." The inclination of the religiously sensitive man to take only the divine or ultimate norm as authoritative may be said to be universal. In the mystic tradition, which Aldous Huxley defines as the "perennial philosophy," the self tries to escape the finiteness of the historic self and to rise to union with the divine self, thus transforming itself from finiteness to nonhistorical absoluteness. In this form the religious impulse is clearly vertical and is in conflict with the impulse toward community. For in that impulse the self seeks to complete itself, as it were, horizontally in its creative relations to its fellows. The community, whether of family, clan, nation or culture, completes the fragmentary and finite self and enlarges it. Obviously, the impulse toward the community cannot be satisfied too consistently because all communities of history are both less and more than the self. They are less because they are more closely bound to nature and necessity than the individual. They have finite and contingent ends for which they claim unconditioned devotion of the individual. In short, they tend to be idolatrous and to usurp the place of the divine. The self always transcends these collective ends, not only in its religious striving but in all its artistic and cultural ambitions. It envisages ends which are not immediately serviceable to the community, though the community is enriched by the multiplicity of these individual aspirations and achievements.

While the vertical dimension of human striving, classically expressed in the religious yearning for perfection, adds depth and richness to communal life, a consistent vertical impulse must destroy the community. For men make life tolerable for each other in community only as they recognize the persistence and inevitability of the fragmentary character of their life. They need each other precisely because they are not whole without the other. Thus men and women need each other and can only be fulfilled in each other. But the religious mystics throughout the ages and in the Christian tradition from the days of Origen have yearned for an "androgynic" wholeness in each individual. They have been particularly embarrassed about the sexual forces in human life and critical of the tempestuous vitalities which were expressed in sex. The consistent religious impulse, which is to say the mystical impulse, has, in short, sought individual wholeness beyond the conditions of historical existence. The desire for perfection is individualistic and not social. It is dangerous to the community not only because it regards the fragmentary and contingent ends of the community as hazards to its pursuit of the ultimate end of life, but because the community can achieve a tolerable harmony only by balancing forces and vitalities in the interest of justice and by exercising coercion in the interest of order. All these strategies assume the imperfection of men in the sense that their virtues betray a residual self-concern which must be beguiled, harnessed, resisted, and, on occasion, suppressed. These strategies are impossible for perfect individuals; for perfection seems always to mean in either the classical mystical tradition or in the perfectionist Christian tradition the conquest of the self over its self-concern, in short, its "selflessness." The justice of the community does not require this selflessness. It requires the expression of competing and balanced vital capacities for the sake of the community.

The desire for perfection must, therefore, invariably express itself parasitically. The celibate disavows the sexual function of procreation in the interest of perfection. The monastics build ideal communities of presumably perfect individuals who have freed themselves of the taint and contamination of the ambiguous institutions of property and government. Both these institutions are necessities of community in a "sinful" world. They are subject to corruption because they both make use of power for the sake of order or of justice but both can be used for self-aggrandizement. The perfect individuals who flee from these ambiguities are necessarily parasitic on the justice and the order provisionally established by these institutions. Perhaps the most vivid display of the contradiction between the impulse to perfection and responsibility for the community is revealed in the perfectionist disavowal of war in the interest of love. War is, of course, an expression of the breakdown of larger community. It represents the effort of the partial community to maintain its integrity against the threat of enslavement or annihilation. At least, that is what war means when it is in the service of justice. But Christian perfectionism cannot make distinctions between justified and unjustified collective violence because any expression of devotion to a parochial community is an expression of imperfection. The self by that devotion acknowledges that it cannot disavow its responsibilities, even if it knows them not to be ultimate.

Thus far we have assumed that there is a similarity between Christian perfectionism and the mystical flight from historical contingency for the sake of union with the divine. This similarity cannot be absolute because Chirstianity is, with Judaism, a religion which strives for historical goals and ends. If it yearns for perfection it expresses the yearning "eschatologically," that is, in hope of the establishment of a perfect community at the end of history rather than for the perfection of each individual who must pay the price of rising above all historic expressions of particular vitalities whether individual or collective.

If we return to Christ's admonition: "Be ye therefore perfect even as your Father in heaven is perfect," regarded as the charter of all Christian perfectionism, it must be observed that this is a translation of translation and therefore subject to misunderstanding.

It is obviously a translation or interpretation of the Old Testament demand to the people of Israel "Be ye therefore holy as I am holy." The term used is *Quodesh*. It connotes in its original form "bright" or "shining." It gathers many connotations in the history of Hebraic thought which enrich the original Babylonian root of the idea of brightness. Most of these connotations indicate the "Mysterium tremendum," the glory and the majesty which are peculiar to the divine. If therefore man or the "people of God" are asked to imitate this divine glory and brightness, which is literally speaking an impossible demand, they can do so only by cultic purity, as demanded in the "Holiness code" in the Book of Leviticus; or they can obey the "holy" god by seeking for absolute justice. The prophet Amos initiated the criticism of cultic holiness and demanded justice in the name of the "Holy One of Israel." He demanded, in short, attainable though rigorous historical goals in the name of the mysterious God. This demand for rigorous justice, which always includes an existential sympathy for the poor, the widows and orphans and the oppressed and always prompts criticism of the powerful, the "Elders of Israel," the rulers and judges, lays the foundation for an historical ethic which remains more relevant to all our historic tasks and responsibilities than the demand for selfless perfection. For the emphasis is always on the self's relation to the holy community rather than the self's absolute purity.

It was the demand to holiness which Jesus translated and interpreted. He did so by interpreting the perfection in which man is called upon to imitate God as inclusive love. At least that is the conviction of many New Testament scholars who have tried to reconstruct the Aramaic words and concepts which Jesus probably used and which were translated in the New Testament Greek with the thoroughly un-Hebraic concept of perfection. The words Jesus probably used, were "Let your love therefore be all-inclusive as God's love includes all." While this reconstruction is speculative it is not idle speculation because the words fit into the context of the Sermon on the Mount, particularly those passages in which parochial loyalties are criticized from the standpoint of a more universal loyalty, as for instance in the admonition "love your enemies" and in the question: "If ye love them which love you what thanks have ye?"

If this is the right interpretation of Jesus' demand for perfection, it does not completely solve our problem because love universalism is a legitimate challenge to human freedom, not to be confined to the parochial loyalties of kith and kin which nature and historical contingency create for us. But it does not help us to fit our parochial loyalties into a general and more universal pattern. It shows us the limits of family and national loyalties but offers us no guidance in fitting our loyalty to the family into the national loyalty, or in relating our loyalty to the nation to our loyalty to a community of nations; or in providing such a community with tolerable equilibria of justice and freedom for the various parochial vitalities to express themselves competitively or cooperatively. All these tasks require the pursuit and the discrimination between determinate ends. They require a rational discrimination between competing interests, and they all assume that every community achieves richness and wholeness through the multiplicity of these vitalities, individual and collective. If they are suppressed because they contain an element of egotism or because they seek for immediate ends and proximate goals, the result would be either a mystic emptying of history itself or a totalitarian suppression of parochial interests in the name of a higher parochial and quasi-universal community, usually the nation.

There is, in short, no social ethic in the love universalism of the gospel. For a social ethic must discriminate between various proximate goals, determinate ends and parochial interests. The love universalism of Jesus establishes a viewpoint from which the ends may be recognized as proximate and not ultimate, and the loyalties as parochial rather than universal. But it must be emphasized that this love universalism is not inimical to a social ethic. It maintains relevance to a social ethic by Jesus' insistence that the love of God and the love of neighbor are not competitive; that they are two sides of the same shield. The double love commandment which Jesus drew from Old Testament sources bids us "Love the Lord our God with all our soul and all our strength and all our mind"; but it also insists that the second great commandment, to "Love thy neighbor as thyself," is "like unto it"; like unto the commandment to love God. The vertical and horizontal dimension of life's possibilities are firmly united, and one must observe that they are more firmly united in the Scriptures than in most subsequent Christian thought. For this thought is always in danger of destroying responsibility to the community by making the love of God competitive to the love of the neighbor and by making it the sole guarantee of "selfless" perfection. The definition of perfection as selflessness is derived from the "perennial philosophy" which both Rudolf Otto and Aldous Huxley rightly describe as a universal religious impulse in both East and West: in the East consistently so, and in the West in various amalgams with the biblical viewpoint.

Perhaps the most significant amalgam of the biblical and the Neo-Platonic viewpoint is made by Augustine. He describes the "city of the world" realistically in terms of all of its particular loyalties, its competitions and conflicts. He defines the equilibria of power which are necessary for justice and he rightly derives the order of the community from the security of some dominant power. Here are the beginnings of a social ethic, but it is made in contrast, rather than derived from, Christian principles.

The "City of God" is informed by the *amor Dei*. The love

of the neighbor has an insecure place in the economy of the *amor Dei*. We must love the neighbor for the sake of God and in order to lead him to God. But the love of the neighbor is suspect because it is the love of a creature rather than the love of the supreme object. The perfection of love is defined in terms of the adequacy of its object. There cannot, therefore, be an adequate definition of the double love commandment. The two loves are not competitive in Augustine's thought, only if the love of the neighbor is subordinated consciously and implicity to the love of God. There is nothing in the Augustinian formulation which would recognize a simple service to the neighbor as the service of God. "I was sick and in prison and ye visited me" is a sentiment which has no place in Augustine's thought.

Augustine is more successful in including "proper self-love" in his scheme of ethics. He distinguishes between two forms of self-love: that in which the self loves itself simply and that in which the self loves itself in God. The latter is presumably the kind of self-realization which is possible as long as the self has an object and end beyond itself. This proper self-love is, therefore, a partial recognition in the thought of Augustine of the paradox, defined by Jesus in the words: "Whosoever seeketh to gain his life will lose it; but whosoever loseth his life will find it."

This paradox, which rightly makes self-realization possible through self-giving but insists that every explicit form of self-love must destroy rather than fulfill the self, illumines the fact that the self can only find itself by having an end beyond itself, for the self is too great in its indeterminate freedom to be fulfilled within the self. Augustine understands the paradox in the ultimate dimension but obscures it in any human relation where he is concerned to prove that the creature, including the fellow-creature, is not God and therefore not worthy of our final devotion. This amalgam between Neo-Platonic and biblical thought has the merit at least of defining perfection in terms which do not equate it with selflessness.

The development of medieval mystic asceticism clearly reveals the preoccupation with the self's perfection. The love of the neighbor may be emphasized, but the instrument is almsgiving and the end is to prove the self's conformity to the law of Christ. Bernard of Clairvaux and the Cistercians may criticize the monks of Cluny, who not only conceived the medieval papacy as a universal political institution but amassed and displayed wealth in the process. They may insist on more rigorous rules of poverty and equalization of wealth. But the ascetic rigor never extends to the limit of challenging the social order as the prophets of Israel challenged it. Set in the context of Western history it becomes apparent that medieval perfectionism prompted sentimentality rather than ethical rigor. The result was the inevitable consequence of preoccupation with the self's selflessness and self's futile pursuit of godlikeness by climbing the ladder of humility and charity. The sects of the Protestant Reformation significantly reveal the same sentimentality, though Quaker charity is considerably more creative than the charity of the monks.

Modern sectarian perfectionism is clearly a compound of the universalism of the gospels and the mystic impulse toward selflessness. The interest in personal purity is revealed in the endless debates of pacifists on the measure of involvement in collective forms of justice and (inevitably) injustice which is permitted the Christian without tainting him with collective guilt. The universalism expresses itself in the hope of transcending all particular loyalties, commitments and responsibilities and thereby establishing a universal community or bearing witness to a universal loyalty. In either case the problems of the community, which must be solved by a balance of social forces and by a discrimination of conflicting rights, are not solved. Nor is it possible to ward off the peril of aggression or enslavement from a particular community in terms of this idealism.

We must regard mystic perfectionism as the premature preoccupation of the individual with the ultimate. The religious experience sharpens the awareness of the self of its own self-concern; but without genuine communal responsibilities the self's effort to rid itself of that concern must prove futile. Mysticism is an individualistic effort to escape the limits of the finite self. The effort proves futile because the self can only be drawn out of itself inadvertently, as it were, by its social responsibilities and affections, however suspect these communal loyalties may be from the ultimate perspective.

The love universalism of the gospels is different from pure mysticism because it moves in a social-horizontal, rather than vertical, dimension. Yet it demands a universal love which finite man is incapable of giving. It can only be regarded as a reminder of the indeterminate possibilities of freedom which exist for man despite his finite and parochial loyalties.

9

MYSTERY AND MEANING

"Now we see through a glass darkly; but then face to face." I Corinthians 13:12

"In him was life; and the life was the light of men. And the light shineth in darkness; and the darkness has not overcome it." John 1:4-5

The final question about our existence is whether it makes sense. An obvious answer to that question is that it does not make sense as simply as either the pietists or the rationalists assume. Life is full of contradictions and incongruities, not to speak of its tragic dissonances. They are not resolved either by the religious revelations of the seers or by the philosophers who are intent to reduce the realm of meaning to some simple pattern of rational intelligibility. We live our life in various realms of meaning, which do not quite cohere rationally. Our meanings are surrounded by a penumbra of mystery, which is not penetrated by reason. For our purposes the philosophies of ancient and modern times may be placed in three categories: 1) those which acknowledge mystery provisionally but expect to reduce it to rational meaning by a final venture of rational imperialism—Hegel is the best modern example of this school of philosophy; 2) those philosophies which realize the penumbra of mystery and the limits of discursive reason in penetrating the penumbra—Kant's distinction between the noumenal and phenomenal world is the classical modern example of this rational modesty; 3) those modern philosophies, strongly under the influence of the natural sciences, which regard mystery as no more than a residual ignorance which the progressive triumph of the sciences will gradually eliminate. This third category of thought is at once the most fashionable and the most dubious approach to the problem of meaning and mystery, and to the strange mixture of rational intelligibility, meaning and mystery which confronts us whenever we raise ultimate questions.

It may be helpful to distinguish between three forms of mystery which surround the world of meaning. One has to do with ultimate reality in which thought discerns an abyss beyond its competence. Two are revealed in our knowledge of ourselves, where we directly experience depths of reality which cannot easily be fitted into any scheme of rational intelligibility.

The ultimate mystery about which we must speak is the mystery of creation. Since Aristotle philosophy has sought to comprehend this mystery rationally by positing a "first cause" or a "prime mover." In our modern scientific culture we have assumed that the mystery has been overcome by charting the endless causal chains in the evolutionary process in which things come to be. We have all accepted the scientific maxim "Ex nihilo nihil sit" and are sceptical of every religious notion which regards the idea of creation as a substitute for the scientific analysis of causes. But there is one chink in the realm of meaning and rational intelligibility. That chink is the fact that no previous cause is a sufficient explanation of a subsequent event. Nothing explains the irrationality of the givenness of things. In terms of a homely example, there is no scientific explanation for the elephant's tusks or the porcupine's quills or for the fact that the skunk has an even more ingenious mode of defense than the porcupine. One can give these irrationalities the appearance of rationality by sorting the animals and flowers into categories and tracing their lineage and relationship to other types. But the most searching philosopher of the sciences in modern life, Alfred North Whitehead, in a volume in which he analyzes the relation of the temporal process to ultimate reality, entitled *Process and Reality,* discerns the limits of rationality and posits a "primordial God," a kind of X to symbolize the realm of mystery.

All mystic philosophies of the Orient and in the Occident, the philosophies which have their source in the Neo-Platonism of Plotinus, have partly rationalized and partly acknowledged the limits of rationality by the doctrine of "emanation," which assumes that the temporal world is a corruption or emanation of the more primeval oneness of all things in God. The scandal of creation is thus avoided, but at the expense of regarding the world of particulars on their temporal flux as either evil or as mere appearance. The proposition which lies at the foundation of Western life-affirmation, the doctrine of the goodness of creation, is inextricably united with the doctrine of the mystery of creation. With this mystery thought begins and ends. That is why, when the theologians were challenged to say in what way God created the world, they came to the rationally absurd conclusion that he created it "Ex nihilo." That conclusion may lead to many absurdities, but properly considered, it guards a mystery beyond the competence of reason. We cannot picture God creating the world out of nothing, but that reminds us that we can give no rational account of how the world of particulars is related to the "unconditioned."

We only know that all contingent existence points beyond itself to an unconditioned mystery of being. Philosophical forms of theology which try to digest this mystery rationally oscillate between the definition of "being" in the Aristotelian description of the eternal structure of being and the Neo-Platonic conception of the undifferentiated "ground of being." The absurdities of the primitive myths of creation must not obscure the profundity of the permanent myth which guards the mystery of creation and sets the limits for all rational pursuits which are always in danger of finding the world self-explanatory and self-fulfilling.

The mystery of creation does not impinge immediately upon our experience, and its relation to meaning, therefore, exercises only the minds of the most reflective persons in their most reflective moments. It becomes directly relevant to our experience only as it represents an ultimate mystery of freedom, which is related to the mystery of our freedom, or more exactly to the two forms of that mystery. The two forms are the mystery of our responsible freedom, despite the determining factors upon our life by reason of our creaturely finiteness, and the greater mystery of the corruption of that freedom and resulting sin and guilt.

Both of these mysteries become apparent not only when

we speculate about the meaning of existence per se. They are directly experienced and they remain unresolved mysteries only because neither of them can be fitted into a neat system of rational coherence, through which we try to make sense of our relation to the total world. The problem is always to be sufficiently empirical to acknowledge the obvious facts as we experience them, even though the acknowledgement threatens the rational system by which we try to establish the coherence of things.

Our responsible freedom can be established introspectively because we know that, though there are always previous causes which can explain our actions, we ourselves stand above the flow of causes and are ourselves the cause of our actions, having the freedom to choose between contrasting ends of action and conflicting motives, which prompt our ends. This freedom does not change or obscure the fact that we are also finite creatures whose actions can be to some degree predicted by those who analyze the main currents of determining conditions, whether psychological, economic, geographic or social. Since our political attitudes are in the main determined by our economic interests, it is possible to predict roughly our votes in an election.

Before the election polls reached their present scientific accuracy a well-known journal which invented the polls went bankrupt because it lost so much prestige when it completely failed to predict the voting trend in an important election. Subsequently, the root of its error was found. It used only telephone directories for its sample electors and the names in the directories were not sufficiently representative. More Republicans than Democrats could afford telephones. Since then we Democrats have improved our economic status, but, nevertheless, the polls did not reach accuracy until mail-order lists were judiciously mixed with the directories so that the names represented a fair sampling of the various economic groups. We are certainly determined and one may predict our basic political attitudes on the basis of the maxim, "Where thy treasure is there will thy heart be also." But despite these determining conditions, there is always a dimension of freedom in which we exercise responsibility despite all the finite conditions which may influence our decisions. While the sciences in general are inclined to various kinds of determinisms because it is possible to deal scientifically, or at least statistically, with man only by obscuring the uniqueness of the individual and the unpredictability of his actions, it is interesting that common sense, art and the law never have had any illusions about the fact of freedom. The freedom of man does not fit into any system of metaphysics, but the historians who know that historiography is not only a science but also an art, know this because they have found freedom and uniqueness so obstrusive in the history of man that it made purely scientific accounts of men's actions impossible.

The second mystery about man is equally validated in experience but equally impervious to any system of rational coherence. It is the mystery of the inevitability of man's misuse of his freedom for his own ends. The persistence on universality of man's undue self-regard is so well established that every valid political science must take it for granted. Nevertheless, every philosophical analysis of human nature tends to obscure the fact that it is the self, and not its "passions" or some social temptation or human ignorance, which is the locus of this self-regard. The same eminent philosopher David Hume who, in reaction to the Calvinism of his youth, denied the doctrine of "original sin," also gave a very astute analysis of the universality of this self-regard and declared that while all men were not uniformly selfish, a political system must nevertheless take their self-regard for granted.

One of the really ludicrous aspects of modern culture, particularly in America, is that the idea of the perfectibility of man is so universally accepted (Americans being the only unreconstructed heirs of the French Enlightenment) that those of us who adhere to the realistic interpretation of human virtue and insist that it is not incompatible with the idea of the "dignity" of man, are usually accused of being slaves of a dogma, derived from an ancient legend. If only we were not credulous enough to believe in the tale of Adam and Eve in the garden we might become enlightened and shared the general illusions about mankind, including the illusion that we must not deal too rigorously with the very problematic human virtue, lest we rob man of his "dignity." The simple fact is that his "misery" and his "dignity" have the same root, namely, his freedom. Perhaps an additional word might be said about the sin of man and the more inclusive concept of his "misery" because in that misery, sin and death are curiously intermingled. It is quite obvious that all men die. The universality of death is the mark of our creaturely finiteness. Yet unlike other creatures we do not die with innocent, but only with practised, equanimity. For we, unlike other creatures, are able to anticipate our death, which proves that we are not, as they, immersed in the temporal stream but slightly transcend it.

Man is, in short, in his freedom as spirit and in his im-

mersion in the temporal flux a very incongruous creature.
Kierkegaard may be right in suggesting that this incongruity
can be comprehended only by "passionate inwardness." Certainly even the profoundest philosophies, whether ancient
or modern, do not comprehend it. They usually follow Plato
and Aristotle and equate man's freedom with his "mind";
and coordinate the mind with a world of ideal rational
forms, while they coordinate his "body" to the system of nature. This makes for two very coherent worlds but it scarcely
does justice to the incongruous unity of the human self,
which traverses both worlds and has a mysterious freedom of
spirit which cannot be equated with "mind," though the rational faculties are obviously among the instruments of
man's freedom over nature. It may be significant that the
poets, rather than the philosophers, have dwelt most consistently and eloquently upon the essential incongruity of
man's nature. Sir John Davies, writing in the early seventeenth century, elaborates a persistent theme of the poets
in his lines:

> "My soul has power to know all things, yet is
> blind and ignorant of all;
> I know I'm one of nature's little kings, yet
> to the least and vilest things am thrall.
> I know my life's a pain and but a span, I know
> my sense is mocked in everything;
> And to conclude, I know myself a man which is
> a proud and yet a wretched thing."

The lines remind us of Pascal's description of the human situation: "What an enigma, what a monster, what a worm,
judge of all things, yet the sink of iniquity and error."

No philosophy is quite able to do full justice to these two

dimensions of human existence. As Pascal asserts, the philosophers are inclined either to dwell on the dignity of man and tempt him to pride or to expiate on the misery of man and to tempt him to despair. Pascal finds the only adequate answer to the enigma in "the simplicity of the gospel." It was indeed this problem which prompted him to defy both Catholic and Cartesian rationalism.

The mystery of man's sin is strangely related to his finiteness in the sense that it is not derived from finiteness or ignorance but is rather the consequence of man's futile effort to escape or to obscure the fact of his finiteness. He grasps after the security of wealth and power to hide or to overcome this insecurity in nature and in history. He indulges in the fanatic assertion of the ultimacy of his relative truth because he is darkly conscious of the scepticism and relativism which lurks under his seeming certainties. If one appreciates the symbolic nature of the observation, one can agree with Augustine's statement that "Men fall into sin, which they could avoid, in trying to avoid death which they cannot avoid." The mystery of the evil in man does not easily yield to rational explanations because the evil is the corruption of a good, namely, man's freedom. The universality of man's excessive self-regard is also a mystery because it does not follow as a natural consequence of his finiteness, though it is occasioned by the juncture of man's freedom and finiteness.

Here, then, are three mysteries, one about God and two about man, which do not fit easily into a system of meaning and which do not yield to a system of rational coherence at all.

All religions try to assert some meaning in the realm of mystery or they stand in awe before mystery and let it discount all the particular finite and limited meanings by which men seek to make sense out of their life. The classical mystic faiths, whether Buddhist or Neo-Platonist tend to warn men that "to name God is to blaspheme him." They are conscious of the hazard of giving ultimate significance to any finite system of meaning or scheme of ends. But in this process they tend to annul the whole historical world with its partial meanings and fragmentary enterprises. They flee from time into eternity. That eternity seems to solve the two human mysteries by affirming the divine mystery. The mystery of human freedom is solved by extricating it from human finiteness and identifying it as one with undifferentiated existence. The mystery of man's evil is solved by identifying it with the particularity of human selfhood. The undifferentiated subject-self emancipates itself from the particular object-self and is thereby redeemed from evil.

Biblical faith, or rather the two faiths rooted in the Bible, Judaism and Christianity, engage in the hazardous enterprise of discerning in some events in history a revelatory depth or height, a "light that shineth in darkness," which are clues to the meaning of history. Christianity goes farther and asserts in the words of the Johannine prologue that all previous revelatory moments are summarized and climaxed in the drama of the suffering Messiah, in the "Christ event." Christianity stands or falls by what Beatrice Webb has called "the ridiculous deification of Jesus." Modern Christians must, of course, be aware that the effort to express the ultimacy of the Christ revelation, in illumining both the human situation and the divine mystery, in ontological terms, after the manner of the early theologians who fixed the "two natures of Christ" dogma, will make nonsense of the dogma.

To transfer symbols of meaning in ontic terms means to commit oneself to the illogical proposition that a man is god. It is illogical because one person cannot be both "passible" and impassible," that is to say both involved in temporal change and transcending time.

But the Christian faith makes sense in affirming that an historic person and event, in the context of the history of Messianic expectations, were a revelation of the divine mercy and justice, and that the crucifixion was the final revelation and symbol of the universality of human sin and the incapacity of men to solve the moral problem of human existence by the strenuousness of their moral striving. If men recognize the fragmentariness of all human virtue, Christ becomes to them the symbol of an ultimate mercy which overcomes the hiatus between human and divine righteousness.

The New Testament is free of ontological speculations. But it does make some ultimate claims for Christ, and upon these claims the Christian faith rests. All these claims are succinctly expressed in the Pauline phrase, "God was in Christ reconciling the world unto himself." It asserts that we have, in the Christ revelation, the sum and climax of all previous clues to the mystery of both human existence and the mystery of the divine creativity in its relation to the purposes of history. If they take the total witness of the Scripture, we could not assert that this was the only "light that shineth in darkness" but the whole New Testament certainly agrees with the Johannine gospel that the most definitive revelation of meaning occurred in the Christ event.

The effort of piety to give a coherent account of the significance of this revelation resulted in the Trinitarian formula, which has been the unvarying basis of Christian orthodoxy. If one appreciates that statements of religious beliefs are symbolic efforts to state the meaning of the revelatory depth in the creative events of the history of faith, we come to the conclusion that the formula of "God the Father Almighty, Maker of heaven and earth"; and of "Jesus Christ his only Son our Lord, who Suffered under Pontius Pilate" implies not some metaphysical statement to resolve the stale question whether or not God exists, but instead it takes the mystery of divine creation for granted and declares the meaning of history has been revealed ultimately and is related to the mystery of creation.

The Christ revelation is, in short, one light which illumines the three mysteries. It gives a clue by faith to the mystery of creation for it substitutes for the unknown X of the primordial god, the conception of a divine source and end of all historical meanings and purposes. Men will seek for a metaphysical validation of such a faith in vain. No degree of metaphysical speculation can ever derive the reality of historical purpose and meaning from the concept of "being." If we believe man's historical existence to be meaningful, we do so by faith and not by reason. For nothing in these structures and symbols of meaning follow in a necessary manner from an analysis of the fixed structures of nature or the laws of logic. Man's life on earth is an incongruity in the context of both nature and mind. If we assert the relevance of a "light that shineth in darkness," we are asserting that certain historic events (and in the case of Christianity, that one historic event in particular) has given us a clue to the mystery of our existence and that our existence is not merely epiphenomenal or an excrescence on nature. We assert that it has a reality of its own, no matter how precarious that reality may seem in the light of the "facts" of nature. We assert that both our freedom in its sinful corruption is real in our experience and that the answers to these mysterious but experienced realities have a status in the total realm of reality.

The love of which the crucified Christ is the symbol, is related to and identical with the mystery of creation. Perhaps this is the "foolishness" of God, which Paul declares is "wiser than men." It is certainly the wisdom of faith; but it does not speculate about uncertain probabilities or affirm propositions of a low order of credibility. It merely closes the structure of meaning on the basis of experience and insists that it is related to the structure of reality itself. The Christian faith rests more on the affirmation that Christ is the revelation of God than on the affirmation that God exists. The "existence" of God is assumed rather than affirmed. Or rather, what is assumed is the mystery of creation which is the ground of existence. The affirmation that Christ is the revelation of God relates the mystery of creation to the meaning of history. But how is history given meaning by this revelation?

If we remember that history requires a meaning by reason of the mystery of human freedom, in which man rises indeterminately above all the coherences of nature and reason, it may seem strange that the "light that shineth in darkness" of Christian faith is not in the first instance the light of meaning for the mystery of freedom, but the light which illumines the second mystery, namely, the self-contradiction in which all human freedom is involved. It answers the human predicament of sin, of the inevitable inclination of man to use his freedom for his own ends, and of the infection of this self-regard in even the highest reaches of moral endeavor, even when they are particularly designed to overcome or to obscure this self-regard, with an assurance that the variance between human goodness and the divine, which cannot be overcome by man, has been overcome by God in his taking the sins of man upon himself. This is the significance of the "good news" that "God was in Christ reconciling the world unto himself." It is clear that the New Testament faith has discerned meaning in a drama of history involving the innocent suffering and death of one who stood under the "Messianic" aura. He was therefore expected to clarify the insecurities and to overcome the moral ambiguities of history by the clear victory of the righteous over the unrighteous as the culmination of the meaning of history. He clarified history in another way than was intended. Everything that is best in history is discovered under this light to be involved in the tragedy of innocent suffering. The moral ambiguity of history cannot be overcome by even the most strenuous moral striving. It is overcome only by God in the sense that the severity of his judgements is matched by his mercy. And of that mercy the crucified Savior is the relevation and the symbol.

Many a sophisticated modern will believe that this tale of God becoming man and suffering upon a cross is a tale for the credulous and unsophisticated but certainly has no "clue" for those who are not even sure whether or not there is a God. But if they will cease to speculate about unanswerable metaphysical problems and make an honest effort to deal with the mysterious but universally experienced human dilemmas, they may find that the idea of a suffering and therefore merciful God is a clue to the meaning of existence.

It clears up two problems about man's self-regard. It does not regard this phenomenon a normative even though it be universal. That is to say, it insists on taking sin seriously and repudiates all theories which regard egotism as harmless because it is natural; or which regard it as harmful but do not see that the universal characteristic of human behavior is not a normative expression of the human self. The other problem which is clarified is the problem of what to do about this persistent and universal human egotism. That is answered on the ultimate level by divine forgiveness. It must be answered on all proximate levels of statecraft by providing all kinds of guards against the dangers of both collective and individual egotism.

There is, in short, neither sentimentality nor cynicism in the wisdom which comes from this "light that shineth in darkness." The Christian faith in its classical form is not related to all forms of utopian idealism, which with boring reiteration declare that all our problems would be solved if only we could persuade selfish men to be unselfish. But on the other hand, the faith of the New Testament does not regard the excessive self-regard of men as "natural." It insists that the inclination of men to make themselves their own ends is a corruption of the freedom which makes it necessary to find their end beyond themselves. In short, the Christ revelation persuades us both to recognize the seriousness of the sin of self-worship and to admit the inability of any righteous man to escape the sin by the rigor of his striving.

There is, of course, a provisional answer to the human problem in rigorous discipline and in doing "one's duty," that is in the kind of moral rigor which Kant, among others, recommended. But there is no final salvation for the problem of the rebellion of the self against the ultimate scheme of meaning by subordinating the anarchy of the "passions" to the rational ends of the coherent self. For the reason, which disciplines the passions, is itself the tool, and not the master, of the rebellious and self-seeking self. The problem of human egotism is, in short, serious and persistent. All psychiatric solutions for particular neurotic forms of self-regard, and all rational schemes for disciplining the reason so that it will seek its own only if its end can be fitted into a coherent scheme of ends, and all political schemes for abolishing particularly vicious and obvious forms of injustice are proximate but not ultimate solutions of the problem. All psychiatric or educational or political schemes for making human egotism more tolerable are valid and helpful if they are not made into schemes of final salvation. They are harmful if they pretend to redeem man ultimately from his evil. Needless to say that any religious scheme with such pretensions of salvation is equally harmful. The Christian faith, in its New Testament form, explicitly fails to make a radical distinction between the righteous and the unrighteous and declares that "all have sinned and fallen short." This insistence on the universality of the corruption of freedom is attested by our experience with both the Godly and the ungodly. But it is regarded as a scandal by both the pious and impious who think that either their belief or their unbelief is the guarantee of their virtue.

The "light that shineth in darkness" reveals not only the universality of sin but the moral insolubility of this moral dilemma. The assurance of divine mercy is the only solution for the problem revealed by the rigor of the divine judgment. It is clear that the light of revelation clarifies not some obscure mystery about the world, but relates the mystery of creation to an answer of a human problem which we know well enough in experience but are reluctant to accept. The fact that we can have an easy conscience only as forgiven sinners who do not deceive ourselves and try desperately to appear better than we are, is a fact which offends the reason only of those who have excluded from the realm of rationality all the mysteries and meanings of man and his history. But it does offend the self-esteem of all idealists who regard the human dilemma as a remedial difficulty which could be cured by a psychiatric, moral, educational or religious program.

The revelation in Christ thus clarifies the human predicament which we have defined as the mystery of man's misery. But what about the mystery of his freedom? This mystery is really antecedent to the mystery of his misery and, in popular esteem, the answer to this mystery in making love the norm of freedom is really the primary content of the Christian faith. Liberal Christianity, in fact, sought to overcome the embarrassment about both the deification of a man and about the pessimistic implications of the main burden of the gospel message, that it presented the "love of Christ" simply as the ultimate norm of human conduct. If the Christian faith were a form of moral idealism and did not clarify the human situation of the contradiction between love and self-love so rigorously, this might have been an adequate interpretation.

But it is significant that even in Pauline interpretations of the Christ in which the message of reconciliation between God and man is given primacy, Christ is no less rigorously defined as the "second Adam" and the perfect self-giving love of the cross is presented as the norm of human conduct. Thus we read in Ephesians 5:1, "Be ye followers of God as dear children; and walk in love, as Christ loved us and gave himself up for us, a fragrent offering and sacrifice to God."

There are two difficulties with the Christian acceptance of

the sacrificial love of Christ as the final norm of conduct. One is that insofar as the love of the neighbor is the obvious norm of human freedom and can be validated by any rigorous analysis of the human situation, it does not seem to require the acceptance by faith of a particular revelation. Stoic and Buddhistic idealism, not to speak of modern forms of naturalistic humanism (Erich Fromm's *The Art of Loving* is to the point here), all agree that man cannot realize himself within himself and must constantly fulfill himself beyond himself in others, in the community and in his creative responsibilities. Why should we engage in hazardous acts of faith when the daylight of common experience can enlighten our darkness?

The second difficulty is that sacrificial love, as exemplified by the love of Christ, the *agape* of the New Testament, is too pure to be a guide for the ordering of the affairs of the community. These require the norms of justice and the mutualities of *philia* rather than the pure transcendence over self of the New Testament *agape*. It is, in short, very difficult, if not impossible, to construct an adequate social ethic, requiring a careful calculation of competing rights, from an *agape* ethic. This is one of the many reasons why both Catholic and Protestant forms of Christianity have had difficulty in coming to terms with the problems of man's collective existence and why Catholicism has been rather more sophisticated than Protestantism in its social ethic. For it frankly applied an Aristotelian ethic of natural law and of justice to the collective problems of mankind and relegated the perfectionist ethic of the New Testament to the monastery or defined its demands as "counsels of perfection."

Clearly the life of the community requires the give and take of competitive striving, the calculations of justice, and the mutualities of family and community for its proper order and health. Any effort to solve these collective problems by the hope that sacrificial love will change the stubborn nature of men and shame other people into the goodness which the saint has achieved or thinks he has achieved, is bound to be reduced to sentimentality in the end. Sometimes, as in the sixteenth- and seventeenth-century Sectarian Utopianism, it tried to guard against disillusion by utopian hopes, which were inevitably disappointed in the end. Sacrificial love is clearly not as simple a possibility as either sectarian Christianity or modern liberalism assumes.

It is nevertheless necessary to preserve the ultimate norm as exemplified in the "love of Christ" for the moral life of man, not as a simple possibility, as liberal Christianity would have it, or as a "counsel of perfection," which may be added to the basic norm of justice for those "who are able" (Aquinas), but as a symbol of the indeterminate possibilities of love in which human freedom stands; and of the transcendent or "eschatological" pinnacle of the ethical life of man. Any scientific description of the human situation or the structure of man's personality of the kind which Erich Fromm attempts, is bound to cut off this pinnacle by some standard of prudence or some estimate of ordinary conduct. Yet the universal reverence for the heroic act and for the martyr's sacrifice, particularly the sacrifice of his life, attest to the universal acceptance of the validity of the transhistorical tangents of the meaning of our existence and to the realization far beyond the confines of any faith, that it is possible for man to lose his life, or his real self by trying too desperately to preserve his physical life, or in other words, that man is sufficiently self-transcendent to know that physical life can be bought at too high a price. This knowledge makes nonsense of all purely utilitarian or hedonistic or even eudaemonistic estimates of the ends of life.

It must be clear that a faith, which accepts a drama of history as the clue to the mystery of divine and human freedom and to the enigma of the inevitable historic corruptions of that freedom, deals with facts of common experience and is therefore merely a vain speculation about insoluble mysteries. It is equally clear that it is not primarily an ontological or metaphysical system. It is not a "science of being" because a science cannot deal with incongruities and mysteries which cannot be mastered by the use of logic and mathematics in guiding the observation and experience of the events of the world. A Christian faith if it is not to degenerate into obscurantism, as it frequently does, must avail itself of all precise, logical and mathematical instruments whenever it has to deal with those aspects of reality which can be measured and sorted and in which meaning is identical with rational coherence.

But it must also recognize that the realm of meaning, which borders on the one side on the realm of rational intelligibility, borders on the other side on mystery. If faith discerns clues of meaning in mystery it cannot pretend to construct a new metaphysics, except as it affirms the limits of metaphysical speculations. The only way of validating such a faith is to bear witness to it in life. The Professor of Moral Philosophy in Cambridge University, R. B. Braithwaite, who has sought to vindicate religious belief in the light of the wholesome scepticism which has been the fruit of the "logical analysis" which has become the chief concern of English philosophers, has come to the conclusion that the only way of validating the Christian faith is by the witness of "living in an agapeistic way."[1] Aside from the fact that the New Testament concept of love (*agape*) cannot be used as an adjective without offending the aesthetic sense, Professor Braithwaite is wrong only in one respect in this affirmation. He has reduced the Christian faith to the simple moral proposition that "God is love" and that we ought to love one another. The Christian faith is more profound than this kind of moral idealism. It declares that God is love and that his love is the final source of harmony for men who know they ought to love one another but who really love themselves. The faith is an answer to their moral predicament and becomes meaningless if the predicament is not known.

The love which must validate the faith is therefore the love which is derived from the realization of the universality of the predicament of self-contradiction (which knowledge draws the fangs of self-righteousness, which are the chief instruments of the sinful self) and from the gratitude that we are forgiven if we freely confess our involvement in the general sin of mankind.

It is an interesting commentary on the religious life that the world knows the religious person, not primarily by his tolerance or spirit of charity, but by his fanatic zeal. This proves that conventional Christianity does not usually produce a piety which has explored the tragic mysteries of human existence. But it is certainly ironic that modern irreligion, beginning with the French Revolution and ending in the communist one, having attributed fanaticism to the "superstitions" of historic religions, which is abolished, then proceeded to enfold a dangerous fanaticism in the name of "rea-

[1] See *An Empiricist's View of the Nature of Religious Belief*, Cambridge University Press, 1956.

son" or of "democracy" or "justice." It proved thereby that we are dealing with a more universal human corruption than the corruptions of a faith which has not understood or appropriated the real meaning of its own faith.

All of history proves that it is as difficult for rational men to be reasonable as for pious men to be charitable. The final criterion of any piety is whether it knows why this should be so.

The clue to the meaning of human existence is verified whenever men witness to that meaning by lives of tolerance and charity, prompted by the consciousness that they are infected by a universal inclination to make more of themselves than they ought, and therefore distrustful of their own virtue, sceptical about their apprehension of the truth and grateful for the love which other men give them, despite their obvious weaknesses. When this initial humility is lacking, religious faith easily prompts fanaticism and tempts the pious and the impious to charge each other with sole responsibility for a common human disease.

The "light that shineth in darkness" can only shine by the witness of those who have used the light to disclose the dark labyrinths of the human heart and have been prompted by the discovery not to despair but to a charitable and tolerant attitude toward their fellow men. The self-deception of the righteous, whether godly or godless, is the chief engine of evil in the world. True self-knowledge delivers the self from cynicism in regard to the neighbor because it discerns the similarity between the corruption in the heart of the neighbor and the heart of the self. It is from such "pessimism" that gratitude and charity flow, provided that there is an assurance of final forgiveness for the ineradicable evil in the human heart.

That assurance can lift the self from despair to "newness of life." In that sense the "light that shineth in darkness" is the final answer to the mystery of human existence, but one which cannot be simply learned as a speculative proposition. It must be appropriated in inner experience and must bring forth "fruits mete for repentance."

INDEX OF PROPER NAMES

Adam, pp. 129, 139
AFL, p. 83
Africa, African, pp. 5, 51, 52, 56, 57, 65, 66
Agape, pp. 93, 104, 140, 143
Algeria, Algerian, Algerians, p. 73
America, American, Americans, pp. 3, 5, 6, 7, 8, 9, 10, 11, 14, 15, 16, 18, 24, 26, 27, 29, 30, 31, 32, 33, 35, 36, 39, 40, 43, 44, 46, 54, 67, 71, 75, 76, 77, 78, 79, 88, 90, 94, 129
"American Way of Life," p. 26
Amos, p. 117
Anti-Christ, pp. 19, 100
Arab, Arabs, pp. 109, 110
Aramaic, pp. 103, 117
Aristotelian, Aristotle, pp. 67, 90, 92, 124, 126, 130, 140
Aryan, p. 88
Asia, Asian, pp. 2, 5, 18, 29, 40, 45, 48, 50, 51, 52, 56, 57, 59, 64, 66
Augustine, Augustinian, pp. 105, 119, 120, 131

Balkans, p. 111
Baptist, p. 8
Baron, Salo, p. 89
Barth, p. 102
Ben-Gurion, p. 109
Bernard of Clairvaux, pp. 93, 121
Bible, pp. 17, 20, 132
Bill of Rights, pp. 78, 79, 80, 84
Bismarck, p. 53
Bonapartist, p. 72
Braithwaite, R. B., pp. 142, 143
Brest-Litovsk, p. 49

Britain, British, pp. 3, 26, 28, 29, 30, 42, 57, 71, 72, 75
Brunner, E., p. 93
Buber, M., pp. 93, 98, 100, 104, 110
Buddhist, Buddhistic, pp. 132, 140
Burke, Edmund, pp. 71, 74

Caesar, p. 69
Calvinism, Calvinistic, pp. 75, 129
Cartesian, p. 131
Case, Shirley J., p. 102
Catholic, Catholicism, pp. 10, 72, 83, 84, 86, 88, 102, 111, 131, 140
Catholic Christianity, pp. 68, 140
Catholic Church, pp. 83, 84
Charles I, p. 44
Children of Israel, p. 84
China, Chinese, pp. 18, 49, 51, 57
Chinese Confucianism, p. 51
Christ, pp. 19, 21, 23, 44, 87, 92, 96, 98, 99, 100, 101, 102, 103, 104, 105, 107, 108, 113, 116, 117, 118, 119, 120, 121, 132, 133, 134, 135, 136, 137, 139, 140, 141
Christian, Christianity, Christians, pp. 1, 8, 9, 16, 20, 21, 23, 32, 44, 67, 68, 70, 82, 86, 87, 88, 89, 90, 91, 92, 93, 94, 95, 97, 98, 99, 100, 101, 103, 104, 105, 106, 107, 108, 109, 110, 111, 114, 115, 116, 119, 121, 132, 133, 134, 135, 137, 138, 139, 141, 142, 143
Christian Church, p. 102
Christological, p. 100
Churchill, pp. 15, 52

Cicero, p. 67
Cistercians, p. 121
"City of God," p. 119
Civil War, The, pp. 78, 85
Cluny, p. 121
Cold War, The, p. 37
Communism, Communist, Communists, pp. 2, 29, 37, 44, 45, 46, 47, 48, 49, 50, 51, 52, 54, 57, 58, 59, 65, 72, 77, 143
Comte, A., p. 17
Conant, J. B., p. 35
Congress, p. 15
Constitution, The, p. 81
"Council of Judaism," p. 111
Cromwell, Cromwellian, pp. 44, 67, 69, 74
Cromwellian England, p. 100
Cromwellian Revolution, pp. 71, 73, 74
Czarism, Czars, pp. 43, 50

Das Kapital, p. 45
Davies, Sir John, p. 130
Declaration of Independence, p. 76
Democratic Party, p. 28
Democrats, p. 127
Deutero-Isaiah, p. 99
"Diggers," p. 69
Divine, pp. 20, 21
Dodd, C. H., p. 102

East, The, pp. 58, 119
Eisenhower, Dwight D., pp. 15, 21
England, English, Englishmen, pp. 7, 68, 69, 70, 71, 73, 74, 142
English Revolution, The, p. 74
Enlightenment, The, pp. 8, 9, 13, 33, 67, 68, 71, 129
"Essay on Liberty," p. 69
Europe, European, Europeans, pp. 2, 3, 7, 8, 9, 10, 15, 18, 24, 26, 28, 31, 35, 41, 42, 45, 46, 48, 51, 52, 54, 57, 68, 76, 78
Eve, p. 129

"Fifth Monarchy," p. 44
First Isaiah, p. 101

First World War, pp. 41, 42, 43, 46, 54
Fourteenth Amendment, p. 80
"Fourth monarchy," p. 44
France, French, Frenchmen, pp. 8, 16, 29, 44, 47, 67, 69, 70, 71, 72, 73, 75, 76
French Empire, p. 57
French Enlightenment, pp. 3, 29, 67, 68, 129
French Revolution, The, pp. 12, 67, 71, 74, 143
Fromm, E., pp. 140, 141

Genesis, p. 101
Gentile, Gentiles, pp. 88, 89, 90, 91, 108
German, Germans, Germany, pp. 42, 49, 53, 95
God, Godly, pp. 1, 2, 6, 16, 69, 92, 96, 97, 100, 103, 107, 108, 117, 119, 120, 121, 125, 126, 131, 132, 133, 134, 135, 136, 138, 139, 143
Gollancz, Victor, p. 104
Graham, Billy, pp. 20, 21
Greece, Greek, pp. 63, 67, 87, 92, 99, 103, 117

Halakah, p. 104
Hebraic, pp. 108, 116, 117
Hebraic Messianism, p. 101
Hegel, Hegelian, pp. 44, 124
Hellenic, p. 108
Herberg, Will, p. 10
History of the Russian Revolution, p. 47
Hooker, Richard, p. 74
Hume, D., p. 129
Huxley, A., pp. 17, 113, 119

India, p. 57
Ireton, p. 74
Irish, p. 111
Israel, pp. 92, 96, 99, 107, 116, 121
Israel, State of, pp. 109, 110
Italy, p. 47

Jacobin, p. 72
Japanese, p. 54
Jefferson, p. 42
Jesus, see Christ
Jew, Jewish, Jewry, Jews, pp. 10,
31, 86, 87, 88, 89, 90, 91, 93,
94, 95, 96, 97, 98, 99, 100, 101,
102, 104, 106, 107, 108, 109,
110, 111
Johannine, pp. 98, 105, 132, 133
Judaeo-Christian, p. 51
Judaism, pp. 88, 98, 99, 100, 101,
103, 104, 105, 106, 107, 108,
109, 116, 132
Jus Gentium, p. 68
Jus Naturale, p. 67

Kant, I., pp. 124, 137
Kerensky, p. 43
Khrushchev, p. 50
Kierkegaard, p. 130
Kingdom of God, pp. 9, 100, 101

Latins, p. 111
Lenin, Leninism, pp. 47, 48, 49,
50, 52, 53
Levellers, pp. 69, 73
Leviticus, Book of, p. 117
Locke, p. 74
Lord, The, pp. 74, 119
Luther, Lutheran, pp. 68, 88, 93

McCarthy, Senator, p. 15
Mahayana Buddhism, p. 95
Manchester, p. 53
Mao, p. 49
Mary II, p. 74
Marx, Marxism, Marxist, pp. 18, 29,
43, 44, 45, 46, 47, 48, 49, 50, 51,
57, 65
Matthew, p. 102
Medieval Europe, pp. 86, 89
Messiah, Messianic, Messianism, pp.
40, 45, 49, 98, 99, 100, 109, 132,
133, 136
Methodist, p. 8
Middle Ages, p. 89
Mill, J. S., p. 69

Milton, p. 69
Moses, pp. 102, 105

Nazi, Nazis, Nazism, pp. 59, 86,
109, 110
Negro, Negroes, pp. 76, 78, 79, 80,
81, 83, 88, 94, 107
Negro Christians, p. 82
Neo-Platonic, Neo-Platonism, Neo-
Platonist, pp. 119, 121, 125, 126,
132
"New Deal," p. 95
New Testament, The, pp. 100, 101,
104, 105, 113, 117, 133, 136,
137, 138, 140, 143
Nicene Creed, The, p. 99
North Africa, p. 73
North European ("Nordic") p. 111
Northern Ireland, p. 111

Occident, p. 125
Old Testament, The, pp. 89, 92,
102, 103, 105, 116, 119
Orient, pp. 51, 52, 125
Origen, p. 114
Orthodox (Christianity), p. 111
Otto, R., p. 119

Palestine, p. 109
Pascal, pp. 130, 131
Paths to Utopia, p. 100
Paul, Pauline, pp. 9, 87, 99, 101,
104, 105, 133, 135, 139
Pauline Christianity, p. 105
Philia, p. 140
Plato, pp. 17, 130
Plotinus, p. 125
Poland, p. 90
Pontius Pilate, p. 134
Process and Reality, p. 125
Protestant, Catholic, Jew, p. 10
Protestant, Protestantism, pp. 10, 20,
21, 31, 83, 84, 86, 88, 93, 102,
107, 111, 140
Protestant Christianity, p. 140
Protestant Church, p. 84
Protestant Reformation, pp. 68, 121
Puritanism, p. 11

Quaker, p. 121
Quodesh, p. 116

Reformation, pp. 16, 21, 41, 68, 105, 121
Renaissance, pp. 16, 41
Republican, Republicans, pp. 20, 127
Restoration, The, pp. 71, 74
Roman, Romans, pp. 58, 67, 98
Roman (Christianity), p. 111
Roman Stoics, The, p. 67
Roosevelt, Rooseveltian, pp. 15, 28, 30, 53, 54
Rosenwald, J., p. 94
Rosenzweig, F., p. 108
Russia, Russian, Russians, pp. 15, 18, 39, 40, 41, 42, 43, 44, 47, 50, 51, 58, 59, 90
Russian Empire, p. 49
Russian Revolution, The, p. 12

Saltmarsh, John, p. 74
Scots-Irish, p. 111
Scripture, Scriptures, pp. 69, 119, 133
Second Isaiah, p. 99
Secretary of State, p. 40
Sectarian Utopianism, p. 141
Security Council, p. 14
Senate, p. 43
Seneca, p. 67
Sermon on the Mount, pp. 101, 102, 117
Sermon on the Mount, p. 102
Slavs, p. 111
Smith, Adam, p. 69
Son of Man, p. 100
South, Southern, pp. 80, 81, 82, 84
Southern Irish, p. 111
Soviets, p. 52
Spain, p. 86

Spencer, H., p. 17
Stalin, pp. 15, 49, 50, 58
Stimson, Henry, p. 54
Stoic, Stoicism, Stoics, pp. 67, 68, 140
Supreme Court, pp. 76, 78, 79, 80, 81

Talmon, p. 72
The Art of Loving, p. 140
The Gospel and the Law, p. 102
Thomas Aquinas, Thomistic, pp. 74, 141
Toqueville, Alexis de, pp. 8, 9, 39, 40
Torrey, p. 103
"Totalitarian Democracy," p. 72
Toynbee, pp. 95, 96, 99, 107, 109
Trinitarian, p. 133
Trotsky, p. 47

United Nations, p. 17
United Nations Charter, p. 14

"Wealth of Nations," p. 69
Webb, B., p. 132
West, Western, pp. 1, 2, 6, 16, 17, 18, 35, 41, 42, 43, 51, 52, 56, 57, 58, 59, 63, 64, 65, 66, 86, 95, 110, 112, 119, 121, 125
Western Europe, Western European, pp. 16, 17, 42
Whitehead, p. 125
William III, p. 74
Windisch, p. 102
Winstanley, p. 73
World Wars, pp. 14, 27, 33

"Yankeeism," p. 11
Yecer hara, p. 101

Zionist, Zionism, pp. 109, 110